HOPE IS CERTAIN

The Story of a Teenager with Crohn's

KRYSTAL WELK

ISBN (print): 978-0-9898093-0-6
ISBN (eBook): 978-0-9898093-1-3

Printed in the United States

Cover Photo credit: Krystal Welk

ACKNOWLEDGMENTS

There are so many people who have helped me throughout my long journey with Crohn's. Firstly I'd like to thank my family. I want to thank my dad and my younger brother for being there for me when I've needed it most and continuing to support me even now. I also want to thank my mom who was literally there for me every single step of the way. She was beside me in the hospital, by my bed at home, and in the chair next to me at every laboratory and doctor's appointment. Mom, without your love, wisdom, and courage I would not be where I am today.

In addition, I cannot thank my doctors enough. Not just my doctors, but also all the nurses who took such good care of me. Special thanks to Dr. Mitchell Katz. He was everything you could want in a specialist and more, and he helped me when I was in critical condition. I would like to thank his nurse, Nancy, who was an angel in disguise. Also thanks to Dr. Marla Dubinsky and Dr. Beverly Hendrickson for all of their medical guidance. These two doctors collaborated with Dr. Katz in an effort to help move me towards remission. Lastly, I had the great fortune of being under Dr. Elizabeth Mannick's care when I moved to Maui. I want to thank her for helping me achieve and maintain health. She has always looked out for my best interest, and has supported me fully in this project. I am so blessed to have been under the care of each one of these doctors. They helped transform me from the sick little eight year old girl in a hospital bed, to the thriving person I am today.

I'd also like to thank all of my friends. To all my friends in California, thank you so much for everything. You were all there for me when I was first diagnosed and hospitalized. Every visit in the hospital, every smile, and every meal you made, meant the world to me. And thanks to my classmates and neighbors for helping me out with school when I first came home from the hospital and in the months to come. Thank you also to all my dear friends in Maui, both those who met me when I was still sick, and those that met me after I went into remission. I would especially like to thank Lexi for her friendship, support, and feedback on this project. Thanks to all my other beta-readers as well.

Lastly I want to thank Dr. Maren LaLiberty from the Shattuck St.-Mary's BioScience Program. I want to thank her for reading a *very* rough and raw draft of my manuscript. In addition, I would like to thank her for all she has taught me, and for encouraging me in my pursuit of a career in medicine. She is credited with providing much of the courage I needed to undertake writing this book. Both her and the BioScience Program have fostered my interest in medicine and have added significant value to my education.

TABLE OF CONTENTS

CHAPTER I

WHAT IS CROHN'S DISEASE?

Everyone has secrets they hold deep inside. And we all have pain. Pain comes in many different shapes and forms. In my case, the pain was physical and emotional.

~~~

The gastroenterologist looked at my mom and stated, "Your daughter is very ill. She should be in the hospital, don't you think?"

After that, I hardly heard the rest of the conversation. My mind was full of questions and worries about what my future might hold.

Listening to the conversation once more I heard the doctor suggest, "It might be IBD, but we won't know until we take a biopsy."

The letters IBD meant nothing to me. *What's an IBD? Do I have one?* I wondered.

~~~

If you're reading this book it is likely that you had a day like the one I just described. As for me, this day came when I was only eight years old. Each of us has experienced the fateful day when our sickness was given a name. The name to our common problem is Crohn's disease.

No matter what your current condition, I hope this book will benefit you. If you are newly diagnosed, this book may give you helpful ideas on how to manage your disease and ultimately overcome it. If you have already reached remission, I hope you will be able to look back at your memories and realize you're not alone out there. It is my desire that after reading this book you will have hope and you will know what to do to conquer Crohn's. You can have the life you've imagined; don't let Crohn's stop you from experiencing that life.

For those of you just beginning your journey, let's start with this important question: What is IBD? Let me summarize the answer to this question in a few paragraphs.

Basically, IBD stands for Inflammatory Bowel Disease. There are two main types of IBD: ulcerative colitis and Crohn's disease. IBD is an autoimmune disease in which the body's immune response goes haywire and the immune system attacks the lining of the intestines, causing inflammation.

Crohn's disease was named after Dr. Burill Crohn, who first described the sickness. The main difference between Crohn's disease and ulcerative colitis is that in Crohn's any area from the mouth to the rectum can be affected, whereas ulcerative colitis only affects the large intestine. Crohn's disease has no cure and the cause of it is uncertain. It is believed to be genetically inherited, but the genetics in the disease are complicated and not yet fully understood by scientists.

About seven hundred thousand Americans have Crohn's disease. A statistic from the *National Human Genome Research Institute* states that about 25% of new diagnoses are being made in patients less than twenty years of age. As a young person affected by Crohn's, I was inspired by this statistic to write this book, from my own perspective, to help other young people receiving a diagnosis of Crohn's disease. This book is not for the younger generation alone, but for anyone suffering from the disease. It may also help you better understand someone you know who suffers from IBD.

Crohn's is thought to be caused by a number of genetic and environmental factors. Smoking, stress, diet, and geographical location have been shown to be risk factors of the disease, but the actual relationship between Crohn's and these factors is unclear.

There are many symptoms of Crohn's. These include frequent and sometimes bloody diarrhea, abdominal pain, reduced appetite, and weight loss.

~~~

Staring back at me from the scale, the number sixty seemed to haunt me. I wondered if I would spend the rest of my life being sixty pounds. It had been so long since I weighed any different. Unfortunately, on the days I didn't eat as much, I weighed even less.

Walking to the kitchen I grabbed a water bottle and gulped the entire thing. Feeling like I might explode, I walked back to the scale and stepped on it again. After this desperate attempt, the scale reported I only was half a pound heavier than before. I wanted to cry.

~~~

Aside from constantly worrying about maintaining my weight, I also worried about frequent stools and stomach pain. Having to go to the bathroom all the time puts a damper on your social life. And lying in bed curled up with pain isn't exactly fun. Let's talk about why these symptoms occur.

Crohn's disease is an autoimmune disease, which means an inappropriate immune response is triggered, which causes inflammation. In Crohn's the response is directed specifically towards the digestive tract. Therefore, the lining of the intestine becomes inflamed and swollen. Affected areas in the digestion tract secrete extra water and salt. This cannot be absorbed properly in the colon, and, therefore, the body's waste becomes watery.

Stomach pain is caused by inflammation and ulcers. Ulcers are sores that expose the nerve endings in your intestinal lining and cause pain. Ulcers can also expose blood vessels, creating bloody diarrhea.

With Crohn's disease, tiredness, weight loss, and malnutrition go hand in hand.

~~~

Ring, ring, ring. The sound of the telephone snapped me out of my tired stupor. My mom answered the phone, and the doctor was on the other end.

Sleepy and sad, the last thing I wanted was bad news. Yet bad news doesn't seem to obey people's wishes. It comes when it wants, and today was one of those days. Listening in on the conversation, I overheard my doctor explain my lab results. "Her numbers are high, which means there is swelling in her intestines. Because of the inflammation, the intestines can't take in nutrients, and losing weight and becoming tired are a result of this."

My mom hung up the phone and turned to me. "We need to make sure you don't lose too much weight."

I sighed, knowing what that meant. It was time for another big meal. This would be the sixth meal of today, and, believe me, I wasn't hungry.

~~~

Before you are diagnosed, you start noticing symptoms. A point in time comes when you start becoming aware of stomach pain. You brush it off at first and think it's just normal. Progressively it starts to get worse and happens more often. After that, you might notice you frequently have to go to the bathroom. Then you might see blood. Your parents and friends might notice a change in your overall well-being. You might start to sleep more and feel chronically tired.

There is a day where you realize something is really wrong with you. You don't know what, but you know that it's not normal for you to feel the way you do. For me that happened one day when I was visiting Disneyland. I understand I have not really told you much of my story yet, so I should share with you the events that led up to that day at Disneyland.

In May 2005, when I was eight years old, our white minivan drove across the border from California into Mexico. My family, along with some friends from a church organization, was going to build a house for an underprivileged family.

After hours of driving in rough conditions on small paths, we reached our Mexican destination, which happened to be the middle of nowhere. Our van was no longer white, but instead was caked with mud and dirt. We at last reached a place called Las Flores, but despite the name, there certainly weren't any flowers to be seen. In fact, not only were there no flowers, there weren't any plants at all. All that could be seen for miles was just dust, dirt, and a few makeshift huts.

The family we were going to help lived in what I would call a "trash house." It was hardly a building, and it was made from scraps of material you might find in a trash can. Their house was the size of a small bedroom, and I wondered how the entire family could fit in it. There was no floor to the house, only the dirt on which it was built. A few chickens roamed in and out. The house didn't even have a bathroom.

The bathrooms in Los Floras are pits in the ground. Not only is that an inconvenience, to say the least, but it is also very unsanitary. As a young impressionable child, seeing how these people lived came as a shock to me. The memory of those bathrooms serves as a reminder to be grateful for the toilets we have. Especially now, as a Crohn's patient, I could not imagine having to use a hole in the ground every time I needed to go to the bathroom.

Though the conditions were unsanitary and the poverty deep, I don't think my Crohn's started in the village. I believe it started on this trip but sometime later. We did some touristy activities such as seeing a blow hole and exploring some local shops, but one fatal mistake we made was eating. We had been warned to not eat or drink just anything here. However, the owners of the house we visited were part of a local church and wanted to feed us lunch. I felt obliged to thank them for their hospitality and ate a tamale. Regardless of whether it was the tamale or not, I ingested something that was not good for my body during my stay in Mexico.

Shortly after we returned home from Mexico, the signs of Crohn's disease started to show. The frequent trips to the bathroom, the blood, the pain, and the weight loss all started to appear.

Other people who had been on the trip were experiencing similar digestive problems. My dad was one of these people. However, he recovered within a few weeks while I got progressively worse.

I visited the doctor several times, but she didn't prescribe medication for me. Finally though, she ordered some lab work.

~~~

"I put in a request to get some lab work done." The doctor's voice faded away as my mind raced with questions.

*Lab work? What could that possibly mean? And what does she
mean by having it done on me?*

Once we left the office I asked my mom, "What did she
mean?"

My mom explained I would have to get my blood drawn. I
was shocked and scared to death. Every kid has heard of shots,
where they put something *in* you. The concept of taking blood
out was foreign and sounded unthinkable.

Arriving at the Lab Quest building, we went up the elevator
to the second floor. I sat in a chair in the sterile lobby. Aside from
a receptionist at a front desk, it looked like mostly old people
got their blood drawn! A nurse soon poked her head through a
door next to the receptionist's desk and called my name.

My mom and I followed the nurse through the door, and
I took in my surroundings. There were many "booths" with
chairs and counters so each individual patient could get their
blood taken in privacy.

I clung to my mom as I took a seat and peered over the
counter at all the equipment for drawing blood.

I sat waiting anxiously. My stomach churned with dread.

A tall, dark-haired man approached whom I will never
forget. He was so kind. He smiled at me and asked me some
friendly questions. I was a nervous wreck, which I'm sure was
apparent to him.

"Now, this is called a butterfly," he explained. A small needle
lay on the counter with two "wing" shapes to the sides of it. "It's
just a tiny needle and won't hurt very much."

I couldn't look as the butterfly needle went into my arm.

~~~

When the results came in, they didn't indicate anything severe. And so my doctor insisted, despite my symptoms, I was fine.

After three months I was having chronic bloody diarrhea and had lost a lot of weight. I was so pale and emaciated there was hardly any trace of the former healthy Krystal Welk whom everyone knew. Barely able to get out of bed in the morning, I knew this sickness was getting out of hand. I now had also developed huge welts up and down my frail legs. The symptoms were becoming obvious.

One day I overheard my mom and dad talking about me in hushed tones. They knew something was seriously wrong. I remember going to my room, breaking down, and crying because I was scared they were right.

The day I really realized something was wrong was about a week before I visited a specialist and was admitted into the hospital.

~~~

Kids screamed and laughed and the air smelled like popcorn. I was waiting in line at Disneyland for a ride called Space Mountain. My family and I were celebrating my younger brother's birthday.

Suddenly, I felt a sharp stabbing sensation in my stomach. I doubled over in pain. *What is wrong with me?* I thought.

I told my parents my stomach was hurting really badly. My dad took me out of the line, and we walked towards a burger stand. The cool evening air did nothing to relieve my agony. I sat down at a table with my dad and tried to eat the burger I had just ordered. However, the pain was too intense. I clutched my stomach.

"Are you sure you're not hungry? Do you have the flu? Do you have to go to the bathroom?" he wondered, listing off the possibilities.

The answer to all those questions was no. I knew what each of those things felt like. This pain was something I had never experienced. It was even hard to keep focused enough to answer his questions. My dad was growing continually frustrated with me.

The fear that had begun to build up in my chest became increasingly worse. I wondered what my future held. Before long, all thoughts of the future fled and only one thought remained: *I don't know what this pain is, but something inside me is terribly wrong.*

~~~

About a week later, on September 12, 2005, I attended my first day of third grade. After school my mom picked me up and told me I was going to the doctor's office. We were beginning to lose trust in my pediatrician, no matter how many times the woman assured my family that I was fine. My condition was critical and I needed to see a specialist. So my mom took me to a pediatric gastroenterologist.

When I arrived at the doctor's office, the specialist confirmed our fear. I was in serious condition.

~~~

"Your daughter is very ill. She should be in the hospital, don't you think?" Those were the fourteen fateful words that indicated my life would no longer be the same.

"Thank God. I think it's about time," my mom replied.

The voices faded into oblivion as I stared intensely at the animal wallpaper. Maybe if I stared hard enough all the insanity would just disappear. I wished that were true. I wished I could escape, but the harder I stared the more I realized I was in for something horribly unpleasant. My eight-year-old mind tried to imagine what a hospital was. Bits of what the doctor said could be heard as I faded in and out of my disturbed daydreams. I pictured nurses in white with masks on and lots of strange equipment. Even though what I pictured was more like a scene from a sci-fi movie than a hospital, I soon discovered the hospital was no less frightening to me. It wasn't the hospital building that was horrific, but instead it was the pain I went through from Crohn's disease during my stay there.

CHAPTER 2

THE HOSPITAL

I hope your Crohn's never reaches a point where you have to be hospitalized. Unfortunately, chances are you will have to spend some time there. With that being said, here are some tips to help you prepare, as well as a few stories of my own experiences.

Firstly, you will want to take certain items for your stay in the hospital. Take cozy clothes! It's uncomfortable staying in a clean and sterile environment, so take belongings that will help lessen your discomfort. Often it is really cold, so include some warm sweats and sweatshirts. Keep in mind that these clothes might get ruined, so don't take anything really nice. I do recommend taking slippers, though. Hospital floors are cold!

Also, it may be good to take some snacks with you since the food there is sometimes disgusting. The types of foods you take should depend on your doctor's recommended diet, but often a bland diet is required. In this case you should eat starchy foods like plain bagels and muffins. Some soft foods like bananas are good, as well as applesauce or maybe Jell-O.

You may want to take different forms of entertainment. Your room will most likely have a television and a selection of movies from which to choose. You can also take your own movies, books, magazines, music, and games.

Lastly, it is crucial to include a binder to take notes on the feedback your doctor may supply. It is useful for keeping your lab and test results in one place. Another benefit is that it is a great place to put fact sheets on medications and notes on drug interactions.

So, let's talk about your first visit to the hospital. Almost every Crohn's patient, at some point, has been admitted there. Some stay for months, others for a few weeks, and still others only a couple days. Regardless, the first time you check into a hospital can be scary, even for adults. The first time I stepped foot in one I was eight years old.

~~~

Walking through the lobby, I noticed countless elderly people in wheelchairs being escorted around. People with casts on their arms or legs left the hospital. Other people were hooked up to oxygen tanks.

A feeling of dull fear crept up. I was still numb with the thought that I was "very ill." The hopeful side of me told myself I would stay here and be all better when I left. The other part of my brain warned me I would not be so fortunate.

With every step I took, I was overwhelmed with the fear of the unknown. After checking in at the front desk, my mom led me through the lobby. It was a lot like a hotel. There was a gift shop by which I saw my dad and brother standing. I felt better having them there, but I was still scared. I remember timidly stepping into the gift shop with my dad, who bought me some lip balm, which I clutched in my hand.

We went up in the elevator and walked through the halls. Everything was white. The walls, the floor, and the ceiling were a sterile shade of white. Every couple feet there was a hand-sanitizer dispenser mounted on the wall. I wondered what my stay in this place was going to be like.

Suddenly, I stopped short. I had arrived at my room. The room was white. What a shocker. There was a bed in the center of the room with countless machines surrounding it. Near the entrance there was a bathroom with a shower. And there was, of course, a television and a window at the far end of the room. What caught my attention was the mass of machinery next to the bed. There were numerous bags with liquid in them and many tubes.

~~~

I soon discovered what an IV was. Maybe you remember your first IV, or perhaps not. As I was only eight, it was a pretty traumatic experience for me. I couldn't believe that the needle had to stay inside me. That blew my mind.

The nurse was rather inexperienced, and it took her a painfully long thirty minutes to lodge the needle into my vein.

~~~

The nurse had a strawberry blond ponytail and red lipstick and was rather pretty.

"I'm just going to put this IV in," she explained, pointing to a machine that was hooked up to the needle in her hand.

"They are just going to put it in real quick," my mom agreed.

"And leave it in?" My eyes widened in shock as I processed that information.

My mom told me not to worry and that she had one when I was born.

The nurse inserted the needle. Apparently it didn't hit my vein because, to my horror, she started twisting it around. My tears started to leak out.

A whole ten minutes passed. I could barely stand it. She pierced my other arm. *Is one arm not enough?* The tears were falling freely now. It had now been about another fifteen minutes.

I squirmed in discomfort. The nurse remained unaffected. I wondered what was wrong with her.

I whimpered in between sobs, "Stop . . . it hurts . . . stop, stop . . ." but it was to no avail. After thirty solid minutes of pain, the inexperienced nurse got the needle in my vein. It was only my first half an hour in the hospital and it was already a nightmare.

~~~

I was rather paranoid about needles after that, and rightly so. Don't worry; it gets much better over time. I hardly notice when they stick me now. And of course, it is very rare to get a nurse as inexperienced as the one I got that day. In fact, I have never had that terrible of an experience again.

I had to get a PICC line shortly after my IV line. I was in such a critical condition that the IV simply didn't cut it. A PICC line is a more direct way to get nutrients as well as medication into the body. It gives more centralized access, which allows for treatments that could not be used by the standard IV. The PICC line stands for peripherally inserted central catheter. Essentially it is a slender tube that is advanced up a vein in the arm until it eventually reaches a major blood vessel near the heart.

A hard thing with an IV or a PICC is showering. You aren't supposed to get it wet, which makes for an awkward shower. Although, while you are there, you're lucky if you find time for a shower. You will probably be feeling too lousy to take one. At least that was my experience.

More than likely you won't sleep soundly during your trip. The hospital is a place in which you are supposed to be able to rest and recover. Often though, it is such a busy place that there are many disruptions. Between disruptions from the noise and from Crohn's (bathroom trips), it is difficult getting any sleep at all.

For one, there is a song that is played throughout the building indicating a baby was born. Ironically, it seemed to go off mostly at night during my stay. The song often aroused any patient who was attempting to get some sleep. A couple times I was so frustrated I nearly screamed at the speaker that was in my room. I also had the song down so well I probably could have hummed the tune on demand for you.

Another sleep disrupter for me was my IV machine. The hospital I stayed at had received new IV machines that the nurses had not quite figured out how to use. Every so often (seemingly at night), the IV would emit a shrill piercing sound.

When the IV machine noise sounded, the nurses would scramble to get to my room and attempt to turn it off. I remember when the nurse came in and tried to fiddle with it. She discovered she had no idea what to do with it and ran to get another nurse. That nurse brought a few of her own nurse buddies. For goodness sakes, it was like a nurse party. They all crowded around the machine and tried to turn off the loud noise.

By the time it was turned off, I was wide awake. I'm assuming the rest of that floor was awake as well. I'm sure the patients next door didn't enjoy the frequent noise coming from my room.

Slowly I would try to drift off to sleep and the next thing I knew they were taking my blood, my blood pressure, or my temperature. Now, in a hospital there is no such thing as personal space. The nurses and doctors are in your room all the time. You'd think it's pretty rude to take someone's blood while they're asleep. I'm joking of course; the medical staff worked hard to save my life. I am grateful for everything that they did, but it was hard to sleep with all that going on.

~~~

I opened my eyes, squinting as a flashlight was being shone in my face.

The nurse mentioned something about drawing my blood. The words sounded muted and jumbled to me. The only thing that was real was the sensation in my arm. It was a dull pain, like a bruise from the blood being drained from my arm. There was also that stinging feeling from the rubbing alcohol they used to clean the end of the IV tube.

I wished that it was all a nightmare, but I knew it wasn't. I wanted so badly to go to sleep and wake up again to find myself in my room at home all safe. I wished that everything would go away. But the nurse in front of me did not disappear.

She proceeded to take my temperature. Shortly after that I slipped back into a troubled sleep.

~~~

The uncontrollable urge to go to the bathroom, even throughout the night, is an additional issue with Crohn's patients. I think this is another reason Crohn's patients are often tired and lethargic. In the hospital, my IV machine was really hard to unplug from the wall, but it had to be done in order to make it to the bathroom. I remember trying desperately to unplug it a couple nights while yelling for my overtired mom to wake up.

~~~

I suddenly awoke in the dark room. I had to go to the bathroom, and so I scrambled out of bed. Pulling on the power cord of my IV machine, I couldn't remove it from the wall.

"Mom!" I yelled.

She was crumpled on her cot in the corner, utterly exhausted. Seconds passed as the urge increased. *Tick tock. Tick tock.*

"Wake up!" I screamed. Panic rose in me as I couldn't control the urge.

Tick tock. Tick Tock.

"Mom, please wake up!" Tears of frustration threatened to spill down my cheeks. I was worn out. I was sick of the hospital, tired of constant trips to the bathroom, and I was losing hope fast. This was almost my breaking point. I just wanted to go home.

Finally she awoke thanks to my frantic yelling. She stumbled to get out of bed and pulled on the power cord to remove it from the wall.

~~~

That was a night I will never forget. I hated hospitals. I hated endless needle pricks and tests. But most of all, I hated Crohn's. I wondered when the agony would end. When would I stop losing weight? When would I no longer have to stare into a toilet full of blood? When would I never have to feel the familiar stinging sensation of a needle entering my skin? When would the time come where I wouldn't remember the feeling of blood painfully draining from my veins into those vials? These were questions that I could not answer, but I hoped to God that I would be home soon.

Have you ever heard hospital food is disgusting? If you've stayed at one, you probably know what I'm talking about. Calling the food unappetizing is an understatement.

~~~

I was sitting in my bed staring down at a bowl of soup. To call the watery cold liquid in the bowl "soup" required quite an imagination. I inwardly debated with myself.

To try? Or not to try? I dared to pick up my spoon. *Hmmm, it can't be that bad.*

Okay, let's be honest, this is the hospital, their food is DISGUSTING.

I tried a little bit of the soup. My face contorted, and I immediately dropped the spoon. After I stared despairingly at the watery bowl of cold liquid, a nurse came in the room.

She looked at me sympathetically. "Do you want me to take that away for you?"

I nodded, already feeling sick to my stomach.

~~~

Lying in bed for long periods of time posed another challenge for me. It soon became painful to walk. I remember crying as I walked up and down the hallways with my mom rolling my IV machine beside me. At one point I simply stopped and refused to go any further. Just then one of my classmates showed up and I quickly wiped my eyes.

Perhaps you won't be saved by a friend when you are having a hard time, but it's important to think about something that makes you feel happy or gives you hope. For me, all through my journey, I have clung to God's Word. Reading my Bible gave me a sense of strength and the will to keep going every day. Because, let's face it, my classmate wasn't enough to get me through this disease, but Jesus certainly was.

Anxiety is in the atmosphere of nearly every hospital room. As a patient, I was always anxious to hear what the doctor was going to say. Each time he entered the room he brought news. The news was either bad or good, and depending on the news, adjustments were made. In my case the news was mostly bad, especially in the beginning. Doctors informed me I was one of the worst cases they had ever seen. I had thirteen lesions, and that was only on my esophagus. The sores continued all down my digestive tract.

It can be very easy to get depressed when most of your time is spent sitting in a bed waiting for updates on how you are doing. Often my mind was whirling with negative feelings and thoughts of anxiety, sorrow, and fear.

One way I comforted myself during this period was by listening to music. And by music, I mean uplifting music. Don't get me wrong—I listen to post-grunge and heavy metal music every once in a while. However, when you are fighting depression, you need happy music. It could honestly be anything from piano music to modern pop. Listening to music while in the hospital would help me to relax so that I could fall asleep.

Having friends come visit helped significantly. Just having a friend sit by me and talk with me was wonderful. It helped me forget where I was or that I was even sick at all. It seemed just like the times we had talked before I was sick. Of course, you can't guarantee people will visit you or that they will be able to pull themselves together enough to talk to you. Most people pull away when they see another person in distress. People won't know how they should treat you or what they should say. True friends, however, will come alongside you and help you out.

22

If you remember the time before you got Crohn's, you probably wouldn't have known how to act around someone with a disease either. Before I got Crohn's, I didn't even know what a disease really was. I had no idea what it meant to have a disease or what I was in for. Even for your friends who are selfless and really care about you, it might be hard. They honestly won't know what to do or say. They might also be scared that you are going to die.

On the other hand, make sure that when you ask visitors to come they aren't sick. Some medications for Crohn's can compromise your immune system. It will be important for you to stay away from anyone who is ill. Even a common cold could end up being harmful for your weak immune system.

~~~

The walls were lined with stuffed animals of all different colors. Instead of the former white sterile environment, my room now resembled a fluffy rainbow. Over the past few days, many of my friends from school had visited, each one bringing something to cheer me up.

A nurse stepped foot in my room and gasped. "What? What is all this? This is not sterile!" A disapproving look covered her face.

"She's eight years old. Does it really matter? They're just stuffed animals," my mom commented. After some time the nurse gave up arguing and left the room.

Later on, I had yet another visitor. She was a girl from school. Plopping down on my bed right next to me, she started to cough. She coughed and coughed. The nurse was mortified, as was my mother.

"I'm sorry, honey, you can't be around Krystal when you are sick." The nurse hurriedly had her leave the room.

~~~

Lastly, your being in the hospital will be hard on your family not just financially but emotionally. It can divide your family up, especially if you are a minor. Either my mom or my dad stayed with me all through my admission. This made it difficult for my little brother who was left at home. He got sick with a cold and so he couldn't visit me because my immune system was not functioning properly. He was so sad that he still tells me about how he felt that day.

Not only will your family be sad, but they probably won't know what to do at first. When I was first diagnosed, we had to do a lot of experimenting. My parents caught on quickly, and so did I. I stayed away from certain foods and tried to get a lot of sleep and not get stressed out.

It can be easy to get stressed when you are going through a hard time. It is especially likely because you probably won't know what's around the corner. Crohn's disease appears to have a mind of its own, coming and going when it pleases. It is natural to have fear of the unknown, but it helps to let go of the fear and relax. What is going to happen is going to happen, and you will get through it. Besides, it is easier to think clearly when the fear is not choking you.

I hope that this chapter gave you helpful ideas on how to get through the hospital. If you've already been in one, I hope you were able to identify with some of my experiences. Everyone's stay is a little different, so it's hard to know what to expect. Just remember that it will help you get well.

CHAPTER 3

TESTING

With Crohn's disease many tests have to be done. It's likely you've been through a lot of them. Do the names "endoscopy," "barium x-ray," or "MRI" bring any memories to your mind?

Most Crohn's patients, if not all of them, have had multiple endoscopies in their lifetime. An endoscopy is a procedure in which a long tube called an endoscope is inserted into the body. The endoscope has both a light and a camera on the end for easy viewing of the intestines. About every year, patients get this procedure done to see how they're doing. It can also determine a patient's diagnosis. During an endoscopy a biopsy can be taken. A biopsy is when the doctor scrapes a sample of tissue from the inside of your digestion tract to examine. This will show if you have Crohn's for sure.

Before my first endoscopy, I admit I was beyond nervous.

~~~

I remember sitting right outside the operating room with my mom. My hands shook from anxiety and my breath came unevenly. A man came out and put something into my IV line. I watched as it made its way to my arm and passed under my skin. It felt wrong.

Eventually I started to feel dizzy. The man smiled and told me I was going to go to sleep. The only thing I remember after that is being wheeled into the operating room and having a mask that pumped out oxygen put over my face. My world went black.

I woke up feeling groggy. I was still in my surgery gown. Other than feeling a little tired and confused, I felt fine. My mom was sitting right next to my bed in a chair. I was in the small room outside the operating room that I had been in before the operation.

I glanced at the clock, and to my surprise it was popping out at me, about three inches from my face. I tried desperately to grab it.

"Krystal, go back to sleep!" my mom scolded. "You need to sleep off the medicine."

"The clock!" I exclaimed, "Look, I can almost touch it! It's coming out at me."

"You're hallucinating, Krystal," she explained. "It sometimes happens when the sleeping medicine is wearing off."

"This is so fun!" I exclaimed, still trying to grasp the clock.

A nurse walked by, and my attention focused in on her. She had about ten different bodies. I was amazed.

"Hey look! That nurse has ten bodies!" I yelled loudly enough for the nurse to hear.

It was like having double vision, except it wasn't double, it was ten times. I looked over at my mom and was shocked to discover that she had three nostrils!

"You have three nostrils," I slurred, poking at her face. "One here and here and there in the middle," I giggled.

"Krystal, you need to go back to sleep. Close your eyes." She seemed a little worried, but I didn't care.

"This is so much fun! Can we take these drugs at home?" I smiled goofily.

At this point I think she laughed a little. "No, Krystal, these drugs aren't safe to take at home."

~~~

Before the endoscopy, however, there is a lot of prepping that needs to be done. You have to get all the food out of your system. There are several ways you can do this. The first time in the hospital I had so much diarrhea and was eating so little I didn't have to force myself to throw up. But the second time when I was at my house, I had to drink this nasty fluid that made me vomit.

I still remember the acidic taste of the supposedly "lemon-flavored" poison, as I call it. The drink forced me to throw up. So all day I could not eat anything, and I threw up everything that there was to throw up. I remember the empty feeling in my stomach gnawing at me as the waves of nausea intensified. All I was allowed to do was drink flavored water.

~~~

Yet another movie started as I stared at my TV screen. My best friend and I had rented lots of movies, yet I wasn't paying attention to any of them. All I could think about was the liquid I had to sip through my straw and the nausea. I wondered how many hours it had been since I had eaten anything.

My friend laughed at something in the movie, but I only had the urge to throw up whatever was left in my empty stomach.

I started to pay attention to the film only to have my mind distracted once again by the urge to go to the bathroom and vomit. Different thoughts ran through my mind.

How much more of this do I have to drink?

I think I'm going to barf.

My stomach hurts so badly.

How am I going to survive five more hours of this?

Hours later, my legs were shaky as I ran to the bathroom once more to dry heave. My friend had left, and it was now dark outside.

My mom stood in the doorway of the bathroom. My knuckles were white as I clung to the toilet seat. I saw her sympathetic face as she said something to encourage me. Unfortunately I wasn't focused on what she was saying. My stomach was churning and I was utterly exhausted. It was around one in the morning. My thoughts were no longer coherent. But there was no way I could fall asleep.

My train of thought was disrupted as I vomited yet again. There was hardly anything left except for that horrid drink and stomach acid.

~~~

I stood by the sink. The clock on the microwave read 4:00 AM in the morning. The nausea hadn't subsided until 2:00 AM, so I had only gotten two hours of sleep. I had an early endoscopy scheduled, and the drive would be about an hour. That meant I had a couple minutes to get myself in the car.

I leaned over the sink trying to support myself.

"I'm so thirsty, mom."

"They said you can't have anything to drink."

I groaned.

"Here, just suck on an ice cube, but don't swallow it," she suggested.

I breathed a sigh of relief and weakly smiled at her.

~~~

Before I finish discussing endoscopy, I want to tell you about my latest scope. A week ago I went in again for a endoscopy. This time I tried Miralax. Miralax is a diuretic, but it doesn't cause you to throw up. So this last scope prep wasn't a big deal at all! I drank white grape juice all day until midnight. This held off the hunger and kept me feeling full. Another thing that made it way easier was just not eating a lot the day before my prep. The day before my prep I ate a really light breakfast, and then the rest of the day I just had a little fruit and maybe a smoothie. When my prep came, I didn't have that much food to empty out.

~~~

Drinking my second hourly dose of Miralax, I wondered how long it would take for the effects to hit me. Nothing had happened yet, so I drove down to the beach. Sitting in the sand looking out at the ocean, I was a little anxious. My eyes wandered to the nearby bathroom. It was within walking distance, and I could run if I needed to. My nerves finally subsided. I was relaxed. The waves were small, and the wind was strong, but I got out on my surfboard anyways.

Sea spray splashed me in the face as I paddled out. Sitting up on my board, I looked at the sparkling water all around me. A little wave started to form, so I dropped back down on my board and paddled for it. As I stood up, the small wave carried me for a few seconds before I fell off.

Breaking through the surface of the cool water, I smiled. My beaming smile turned into laughing. *The conditions for surfing are as bad as they get,* I thought to myself, *and it doesn't even matter. I'm out here in the ocean when I should be at home throwing up.*

~~~

Miralax was a huge blessing for me. No longer did I have to stay at home miserable and vomiting all day, but I could go out and have fun. Of course, I'm in remission, so I don't have any pain or diarrhea from the Crohn's at this point. But Crohn's or not, Miralax is much easier. The diarrhea didn't even hit me until late in the day. Eating less the day before my prep was a really helpful thing to do, and I recommend you try it. Less food means less diarrhea.

Moving on, a barium x-ray is another way doctors can see where the disease is. You have to swallow a chalky white fluid that does not allow the x-rays to go through it. So when the doctors look at the x-ray, they see white wherever the barium is. This drink is often hard to take because it makes you feel nauseous.

~~~

Lifting the cup towards my lips, I tried to tell myself it couldn't be that gross. My hopeful thoughts were contradicted when the substance entered my mouth. Coughing and sputtering, I had not been prepared for the foul taste or chalky texture of the drink.

I looked at my mom with eyes that said, *I can't do this.*

After a few more sips, the nausea hit me full force. I'm not sure if it was the taste of the barium or the actual chemicals in it that made me sick. I think the combination of both did the trick.

"I'm going to puke. I can't do this."

"You have to try, Krystal."

My mom looked at the man performing the test. "What happens if she throws up?"

"Then she'll have to start all over again," he explained.

That didn't sound like fun. *I have to do this,* I told myself.

"Focus on something," my mom advised. "When I was pregnant with you, I stared at a spot on the wall as hard as I could."

I looked straight ahead at the hand-sanitizer container mounted on the wall. That was my target. I stared so hard I thought I would burn a hole in the wall.

The "chalk" became increasingly hard to swallow, and my stomach was churning.

The word "Purell" began to become engraved on my mind. I clutched my stomach, holding the drink in my other hand. The cup containing the barium seemed to have no bottom.

Hours dragged by, and I was miserable. *When will it all end? All the tests, all the pain, and all the sickness . . .*

~~~

As you can see, the barium enema was not my favorite test. If you want to be optimistic, at least the barium enema doesn't involve needles.

A test that is not normal for Crohn's but I had done was an EKG. This was done because I was having unexplained chest pain. This was likely because of all the different medications I was taking at once. An EKG, or electrocardiogram, takes the heart's electrical activity and translates it into lines called waves.

~~~

Thud thud, thud thud, thud thud. My heart was beating loudly and quickly. I felt pain in my chest and immediately tried to sit up in bed.

"Mom! My chest hurts. I think there's something wrong."

Getting up quickly, she wasted no time getting a doctor.

The doctor came into the room and sat down. "Well, maybe the mix of drugs you are on is affecting your heart. We'll do an EKG on you."

What in the world is an EKG? I asked this question in my head but didn't dare ask it out loud. I didn't really want to know the answer. I was sick of tests.

During my EKG, I lay very still on a table. Different electrodes were stuck onto me. *What in the world is this?* Worries choked me. I half-expected an electric shock. The screen on the machine lit up with jagged lines. The lines moved up and down with my heart beat. Surprisingly the nurse took the electrodes off soon. "You're done," she said.

I couldn't believe my luck. No needles and no electric shock! As the saying goes, today was definitely my day.

~~~

Another painless test is an ultrasound. This test is normally used for women who are pregnant, and I have to say, this test is actually pretty fun! I know that sounds unbelievable, but it's true.

~~~

"What are they going to do? Does it hurt? Are you sure?" I barraged my poor mother with questions.

"No, Krystal, it doesn't hurt. It's just an ultrasound. I had one done when I was pregnant, and I saw you in my womb."

I wasn't really listening to her. I was really worked up and scared. I remembered my IV trauma and shuddered. The thought of the chalky barium entered my mind, and I started panicking.

Nurses came into the room and started preparing as I silently freaked out. I was practically quivering when they pulled up my shirt and put a cold gel all over my abdomen. I squeezed my eyes shut, half-expecting some kind of torturous thing to take place. But nothing happened. The nurse rubbed a wand over the gel areas, and then I was done.

~~~

This test has to do with sound waves. These sound waves are emitted and bounce off the tissue, creating an echo. A computer can then create an image of the targeted organ based on the echoes. The gel is a conductive substance to help pick up the sound waves. Thinking back on that test, I know my fear wasn't realistic. I mean, what could go wrong with gel? In my eight-year-old mind I wasn't thinking rationally though. And besides, everything was foreign to me. I didn't know about any of this equipment. And more often than not during my stay, I ended up very surprised. So as far as I'm concerned, in the hospital it's safe to assume anything can happen.

Diabetes testing also came as a surprise to me. There is a small white tool that is pressed on your finger and pushed down like a stapler. The needle comes out and pricks your finger. After several fingers a day every day, it gets old.

~~~

"What's that?" I hesitated, looking at the small white device in the nurse's hand.

"We have to test you for diabetes; it just feels like a small pin prick."

Great, more poking.

She must have known what I was thinking because she kept assuring me it would be really fast and would hardly hurt. "Just a little prick" is what they always said. I dreaded needles, but I had to get this over with.

The nurse rubbed my finger with rubbing alcohol and then pricked me. I looked away and winced at the slight pain.

~~~

A few days later I can remember this scene. I was so tired I was almost delirious.

~~~

"They got this one and this one and this one," I counted all the fingers that had been pricked on my right hand.

"And this one they got three times, and they got this one too and this one twice . . ." I began to list off the fingers on my left hand as well.

After I tallied up the pricks, I made a discovery.

"Mom! Mom! They didn't get this one yet! This finger hasn't been poked yet!" I stated with pride.

37

~~~

You know you're not an average kid when you consider experiences like that an accomplishment. Of course, none of my experiences in the hospital happen to an average healthy kid. Guess you could say I was different from my peer group.

I'm sure you've heard of a stool test. This is pretty painless but still by far the most irritating test. It's not complicated at all; it's just not fun. And it certainly isn't anything a kid or an adult wants to do. I don't think I need to explain this test. If you don't know what it is already, I'm sure you'll find out soon.

These are the majority of the tests performed on patients with IBD. Although they are often a pain, just get through them! Remember, once the doctors know what's wrong, they can start treatment. So that's what I want to talk about next: the symptoms of Crohn's and medications used for treatment.

CHAPTER 4

SYMPTOMS
AND MEDICATION

Diarrhea is usually the number one symptom in Crohn's. This is because the inflammation in the digestive tract causes the cells to produce excessive amounts of salt and water. The damaged lining of the intestines can no longer absorb this extra fluid. Therefore stools are loose and watery. Oftentimes, the diarrhea is bloody because of ulcers in the intestines.

~~~

Oh no. I started to panic.

"Get off the freeway," I demanded urgently.

My dad knew what that meant. I needed to use the restroom quickly.

Counting the seconds on my hand, we exited the freeway in search of one. When the large yellow "M" for McDonalds came

39

into view, it was quite a relief. Pulling into the parking lot and running out of the car, I hoped to make it in time.

Surprised customers turned their heads to see me wildly run towards the bathroom. The door slammed behind me, and I locked myself into a stall. Everything was going to be okay.

Walking back to the car, I thought to myself, *I made it just in time once again.*

~~~

Chronic stomach pain is an unpleasant companion of any Crohn's patient. This along with diarrhea is most often the reason people seek medical help. The pain can be due to a number of factors such as blockages, inflammation, ulcers, fistulas, or other complications from the disease.

Fatigue is another telltale sign that something is seriously wrong. This is a bigger issue when you first get diagnosed or when you are having a flare-up. When Crohn's is active, your body will not be able to absorb any nutrients because of inflammation from the disease. It is important to control the disease and reduce the inflammation so the intestines can start to work and your body can receive the nutrients it needs. Anemia can also be caused from inflammation, so even if your intestines absorb nutrition, the inflammation causes anemia.

~~~

"She might be anemic," the doctor concluded.

Good grief, I thought to myself. *Another medical problem?*

"What does that mean?" I asked the doctor.

"It's not a huge concern. Being anemic just means that you don't have enough red blood cells. That's why you might feel extra tired," he replied.

"So it will go away?" I asked.

"In your case it will stop when your disease gets under control."

I breathed a sigh of relief. *That's not too bad.*

~~~

Many other symptoms and complications may accompany Crohn's disease, but diarrhea, pain, and tiredness are probably the three you are most familiar with. Listing these symptoms leads to an obvious question: What can be done to help give you relief?

The medications used for Crohn's disease are corticosteroids, antibiotics, immune suppressors, and 5-ASA drugs. One, all, or a combination of these drugs may make your life as a Crohn's patient much easier! Every person with Crohn's is different and will respond differently to certain prescriptions. However, I believe you can find a combination that will work well for you. Even though these medications can help stabilize your disease, they have their own temporary and long-term effects.

Corticosteroids work to reduce inflammation by suppressing the immune system. They bring down inflammation by lessening the production of inflammatory chemicals. The function of white blood cells is also changed by them. This prevents further damage to the tissue in your intestines from the autoimmune response in Crohn's disease.

Almost every Crohn's patient is familiar with the name "prednisone." Oftentimes this name does not provoke happy memories. Despite the medication's ability to fight the disease, it does have some unpleasant side effects. These effects include nausea, dizziness, chills, hot flashes, increased hair growth, changes in mood, depression, acne, heartburn, tiredness, vomiting, confusion, loss of contact with reality, and sudden weight gain. A complete list of side effects can be viewed online. With the high dose of prednisone I was prescribed, many of these effects became familiar to me.

Here are a few memories I have of them.

~~~

Listlessly I stared at the papers before me and fidgeted with my pencil. I squinted at the multiplication problems on the page. Out of nowhere, a spell of dizziness and confusion came over me. The numbers seemed to swim around in front of me. All of a sudden a drop of liquid appeared, blurring the numbers even more. *Are the numbers actually swimming?* I wondered.

To my disgust, I discovered that my homework was not, in fact, becoming an ocean but that my own sweat was dripping down. My mom took a seat next to me, muttering about how cold it was in the house while she practically shivered.

Standing up, I walked over to the wall and flipped the switch to turn on the ceiling fan.

With wide eyes she asked, "Krystal, what are you doing?"

"I'm sweating, mom!" I yelled, feeling frustrated.

She looked at me like I was crazy while she sat there freezing.

~~~

As mentioned in the brief flashback above, prednisone causes dizziness. This makes it very difficult to function in school. Being dizzy and nauseous and having spontaneous hot flashes is not ideal for a learning environment. When I was first on this medication, I couldn't read anything; all the words on the page were moving around. At times it was hard for me to walk because the world around me appeared to be spinning. I particularly noticed dizziness while driving in the car and had to stay home many times because of it. So this won't just affect those of you in school, but it can affect your driving or job as well. Since I was only eight, all I had to worry about was keeping caught up at school.

If you have a job, take time off. Don't try to force yourself to perform tasks that you can't. It will only frustrate you. Crohn's may limit you when it is active, so just take some time off and be patient. You will go back to your normal self, I promise.

Arguably the most awful effect that prednisone will have on your appearance is known as "chipmunk cheeks" or "moon face." While taking this drug, your face can become swollen and round. Once you are off of the medication this will go away, so don't worry.

Another aspect of this medicine is the uncontrollable urge to eat. My doctor warned my mom when he prescribed it that I would always feel hungry. I can recall that he advised my parents to buy a lock for the fridge. Of course they didn't take him too seriously. He really wasn't kidding though.

My diet was very limited at that point, but there were a few places that I always ordered food. One of those places was El

Pollo Loco, which is a fast food restaurant similar to Kentucky Fried Chicken. My parents would pick up grilled chicken for me all the time.

~~~

The chicken was so delicious. I was sitting around a fire pit eating it off the bones. Even though I had already eaten seven pieces, I was still starving. I picked up my eighth piece, but I couldn't seem to rip the meat off no matter how many times I tried. Frustrated, I tried even harder.

Suddenly I woke up and realized I had been dreaming. I looked down at my hands, which were still tearing at my sheet. *No wonder I couldn't get the chicken off,* I thought.

~~~

Besides the incredible urge to eat, the actual taste of the medication is something I will never be able to forget. Prednisone is a bitter pill, and it is nearly impossible to get the taste out of your mouth. I remember eating a cookie after swallowing one of those pills. Even the taste of the delicious snicker doodle cookie wasn't strong enough to erase the aftertaste of it.

Not only does the drug taste bitter, but it can cause your feelings to play tricks on you. Think of a rollercoaster you've been on. Now think of all the ups and downs of the ride. Prednisone can easily turn your emotions into an out-of-control rollercoaster. It makes your moods change so rapidly that one minute you can be smiling, and the next you can suffer from severe depression.

When I was trying to wean off the drug, I even had a few thoughts of suicide. As hard as this will be for you, it will be equally hard, if not more difficult, for the people around you.

~~~

The colorful posters on the walls at the mall did nothing to lift my spirits. Preoccupied shoppers passed me as I just stood in the middle of the mall. I had no motivation to do anything. Feelings of depression grew stronger by the minute. Nearing a shoe store, I entered it and sat down.

A sales clerk approached me. "Is there anything you'd like to try on?"

In reply to her, I simply started crying.

"I'm sorry; I don't think she's feeling well," my mother apologized. "Come on, Krystal, let's go home."

But I just sat in the chair sobbing. I couldn't move or speak; all I could do was cry. My grief was overwhelming.

~~~

There is hope though! Newer steroids such as Entocort do not have as harsh of side effects. This is because the drug targets certain parts of your digestive tract instead of affecting your whole body. It is absorbed into the terminal ileum and ascending colon. This medication won't work if your disease isn't located in those spots. However if that's where your disease is, I recommend asking your doctor about trying it. Prednisone may be necessary to control aggressive outbreaks of Crohn's, but Entocort can be used for more mild flare-ups. I have used a combination of Entocort and Flagyl to control a mild flare-up in the past. I was very grateful for this medication; I did not want to have to take prednisone again.

Not only are steroids used for Crohn's, but another group of medications called antibiotics are sometimes helpful. Antibiotics kill off bacteria. This can help to stop the autoinflammatory response, since the immune system is responding inappropriately to normal bacteria in the gut. A downside of this is that good bacteria are killed with bad bacteria. You can ask your doctor about taking probiotics to replenish good bacteria to your gut while you are taking antibiotics. Common antibiotics used for Crohn's are metronidazole (Flagyl) and ciprofloxacin (Cipro). However both of these medications can have long-term side effects. For example, Cipro can cause a tendon rupture. I chose not to take this medication since I was a dancer and I didn't want to risk any permanent or even temporary damage to my tendons.

Flagyl can cause peripheral neuropathy if taken for too long. Basically this means your nerves could become damaged and not work right. Be sure to call your doctor if you feel any tingling or numbness anywhere.

~~~

I woke up and glanced at the clock, which read 10:35 AM. Groaning, I got out of bed. Stumbling to the bathroom, my whole body felt numb from sleep. I gradually woke up, and the numbness wore off everywhere except in my fingers. The tips of my fingers tingled. *That's unusual.*

I tried moving my hands around. *Maybe they're still asleep.* But the numbness wasn't anywhere except for my fingers. Exiting my room, I ran down the hall.

It could be the Flagyl, I thought worriedly.

Fumbling with the doorknob to my parents' room, I finally succeeded in opening the door. I shook my mom. "Hey mom, my fingers feel all tingly."

Without hesitation she threw off her sheets and got out of bed. "I'm going to call the doctor."

~~~

Fortunately, I weaned off the Flagyl right away and didn't experience any nerve damage. It's always good to be aware of any risks from medications you take. And if you think you might be experiencing any of them, call your doctor.

Another group of medications are 5-ASA (5-aminosalicylic acid) drugs. Some of the most common types of these used for Crohn's are Pentasa, Asocol, and Salofalk. These medications are used to reduce inflammation. The list of side effects for these 5-ASAs are much milder than those of steroids, and includes things such as hair loss or headaches. I don't think I really experienced any side effects of Pentasa. Since I was taking so many different medications, it was hard to distinguish which one was causing which side effect. These medications are more often used for ulcerative colitis rather than Crohn's.

Lastly there is a group of long-term maintenance drugs. These are meant to be used for a person's whole life. They are immunosuppressive, which means they shut down your immune system so to speak. The most common are 6-mercaptopurine (6-MP) and azathioprine (Imuran, Azasan). Since they suppress the immune system, it is easier to catch an infection while on these treatments. These, however, take six to eight weeks to start working. Patients are put on steroids during this time until the maintenance drug begins to work.

More recently, another type of medication was developed. You may have heard of Humira or Remicade. They can be used for moderate to severe Crohn's. These medications have to be injected through an IV. They are usually injected every two to eight weeks depending on how long you have been on them and what your current condition is. For some patients, these drugs works miracles. There are some serious warnings on the label. There are online studies that show the risk of these side effects occurring, and you can also ask your doctor about this.

One benefit of Humira or Remicade is that, unlike other maintenance drugs, they work instantly. Patients have experienced relief in just twenty-four hours after an infusion. A lot of patients like this option, because they aren't required to take steroids. Teenagers especially choose Remicade for this reason since steroids stunt their growth.

Every case of Crohn's is different and varies greatly depending on the individual. Some Crohn's patients don't react well to treatments. If you are one of these people, there are a few options that might help. I recommend looking into taking different types of supplements. These aren't meant to be a substitute for medication, but could be used to help combat the Crohn's in addition to whatever medicine you can take. One thing that really helped me was probiotics. For me it has been really important to balance the number of bad bacteria with good. Taking probiotics seems to balance the bacteria in my gut and provide me with stability. Acidophilus, which is a type of probiotic, might be something you'd want to look into. It is a type of bacteria found in yogurt and used to help in human digestion. Acidophilus may be beneficial for Crohn's patients.

One article suggests that a specific bacterium in probiotics may help to reduce inflammation. This bacterium is called F. prausnitzii. A study was done in mice with colitis that showed a significant reduction in swelling. The long title of this journal article is: *Faecalibacterium prausnitzii is an anti-inflammatory commensal bacterium identified by gut microbiota analysis of Crohn disease patients.* Search for that on the Internet to find the article. From the research it seems that probiotics may be helpful. For me personally, they have certainly appeared to improve my condition. Next time you go to your doctor, ask about probiotics.

Additionally I have been taking fish oil. While the effects of fish oil are still being debated, it has seemed to work for me. Some people strongly disagree that fish oil is beneficial for Crohn's patients, while others advocate it. This is, again, another supplement to get your doctor's opinion on.

There is also a link between vitamin D and Crohn's. It is recommended for Crohn's patients to take vitamin D supplements. Vitamin D and calcium also help with bone strength and prevention of developing osteoporosis. Patients with Crohn's are at a much higher risk of getting osteoporosis, which is a disease where your bones lose density and become weak. You can have a bone-density test done if you are concerned about this. Just a tip for you: avoid soda. It can take away from the calcium in your bones.

So how do you know which medications to take? How high of a dose should you take? How do you know if a medication is going to work? These are all things you may be wondering if you are newly diagnosed.

Deciding which medication to take should be based on what your doctor recommends. You can also do a little research of your own online. As far as dosage goes, that depends on your height and weight. Your doctor will prescribe this to you. It will also depend on the severity of your disease. It is impossible to know how well you're going to respond to a medication ahead of time. Every individual has a unique chemical composition. It is somewhat of a trial-and-error process. If a medication is causing a negative reaction, you may have to wean off of it.

Chances are you might be taking a combination of medications. All these different drugs have to be taken at different times of the day, or possibly multiple times a day. How can you manage them and fit them into your daily life?

~~~

"Krystal! Go take your next pill!" my mom yelled from across the house.

The clock read 1:00 PM. And nearly every hour I had to take something. "Where's the box?" I shouted back.

"It's in the kitchen!"

The caboodle was on the kitchen table. With thirteen different compartments, it held all my pills. Pills of all sizes, shapes, and colors were inside.

Which one do I take at one o'clock? I couldn't remember. Looking over at the counter, I read a small whiteboard that had my schedule written on it.

The schedule showed, "1:00 PM—Pentasa (blue/green capsule)."

I sighed and popped the pill in my mouth.

~~~

A whiteboard and a caboodle was the way I managed my pills. I had my mom reminding me since I was young. If you are older you might want to set alarms on your phone. There are other ways you can remember, but eventually you will have to memorize your schedule.

Lastly, make sure you are aware of any restrictions that your medications have. For example, with a steroid called Entocort you cannot have grapefruit juice. A lot of drugs do not allow any alcohol consumption. Antibiotic labels warn you to stay out of the sun. So just make sure you know of any restrictions. A pharmacist or doctor can tell you of these and the label will include warnings.

Hopefully you won't be taking as many medications as I was, but if you are, or if you're taking more, don't lose hope! You will probably be able to wean off of many of them. And it is likely that you will reach remission, or at least have times where the disease is mild.

CHAPTER 5

SOCIAL SITUATIONS AND PEER PRESSURE

Surviving social situations can be challenging when you have Crohn's. When you're worrying about stomach pain, taking your medication, and trying to find a bathroom, being social is the last thing on your mind. I cannot tell you how many times I sat at a lunch table trying to figure out what I could eat that would appear normal. Or how many times I've had to excuse myself from class to use the restroom. Or how many times I've slipped medication into my mouth after making sure no one was watching. Keeping up with the energy level of a group is hard as well, and I've had to miss events simply because of fatigue.

To be perfectly honest with you, your life won't stop because of Crohn's. At times when the disease is bad, you might have to put your social life on pause. But you will learn to deal with your disease and go back to living your life. You can still do a lot of the activities you used to do!

The prednisone made me so dizzy I couldn't read. This made it hard for me to do school work as quickly as I used to. I had a lot of friends help me out with my schoolwork. I remember my neighbor friends used to come over and read books to me.

It also made it hard to even walk around.

~~~

The playground seemed to spin. I wished I hadn't come outside for recess. Stumbling across the grass, I finally lay down on a cement-paved area.

"Are you okay?" some of the other kids asked me.

"Yeah," I murmured, disoriented. Their concerned faces seemed to spin as well.

I felt weak and lightheaded. I didn't care about anything going on around me. It was all just a blur. I hoped I would never have to stand up again. I wished I could lay there, numb to everything, forever and ever.

~~~

Maybe you've felt that way. Maybe you've spaced out and been isolated in your own little world, overwhelmed by your physical and emotional troubles. Although blocking everything out is a nice way to deal with things, you can't do that forever. In my case, I had to get up off the ground and go back to class.

Whether it's class or your job, you might need to take a break. I missed tons of school when I was on heavy doses of prednisone. The scene I just described to you was a day I should have stayed home. Don't push yourself to do something you can't do. Patiently wait for relief. You will have better days!

Secondly, eating with people in general is sometimes hard. One thing I have had to deal with this year as a freshman in high school is diet. This is especially hard if you are a girl. Certain girls at school seem like they might have an eating disorder. They are extremely concerned about their weight and it bothers them to no end when you eat healthy and they don't. These girls have humiliated me because of their own issues with their weight.

I learned to get better at simply smiling at other's rude comments. I used to be afraid to eat in front of people. I worried about what they would say. Going to restaurants was another situation I loathed because I wouldn't be able to eat what was on the menu. Now I'm pretty good at putting in special orders and explaining exactly what I want. In all honesty, life is much more than food. However, it is still hard in social situations.

I've had friends shove candy or desserts in my face and try to force me to eat it. When I refuse they resort to teasing me. They'll say, "You're so skinny! You're like anorexic. Stop being anorexic, put some meat on those bones."

Just recently a friend spent the night.

~~~

We were in my bedroom and she was unpacking her bag. First she pulled out Skittles and then some other candies. She threw a few and grabbed a handful for herself. Plopping down on the bed, she popped the candy into her mouth. I picked up the candy she had thrown me, looking at it in the palm of my hand. I knew I couldn't eat it, so I sighed, and gave it back.

"I'm on a diet," I said flatly, hoping she would leave it alone.

She scoffed and seemed slightly irritated. It was as if suddenly all the joy of eating her candy had been taken away.

~~~

This is the same with older people. If you are in your twenties, you will experience the same pressure to drink alcohol. Eating and drinking is a social thing. People go out to eat together; they go out to bars together. And if you don't participate, it can bother people. If you know something is going to make you sick, don't eat it! It's honestly not worth the pain.

Being a teenager these last couple years, I haven't really told anyone about my Crohn's. As a result of this I often feel as if I have to be guarded all the time around people. I can't let them know my secret. I have to ward off the insults and snarky remarks. Crohn's is a very personal disease, and it can be hard to share with others because they simply don't understand.

Even close friends may not understand. They just see you as another normal teenager. You don't look like you have anything wrong with you, so they forget. They just expect you to be like them. This is one of the most frustrating dilemmas. Being misunderstood by others is extremely difficult.

I had a friend during a flare-up who I had difficulty with. I always had to eat a lot of food. I was eating up to five meals a day just to maintain my weight. I also had to rest a lot. My friend would want to keep doing activities, and she could go and go. But I got tired out really easily. And she would get mad and presume it was just an excuse to not hang out with her.

This would make me angry. I would think: *It's bad enough I have to deal with this disease; I don't need to deal with ignorant people like you too. If you don't want to believe me that's fine, but I'm telling you the truth.*

Not only do friends not always believe you, but they forget about your condition. I have to remind them over and over again. I remember having a friend who I had to tell about three or four times. Every time I saw her, I had to explain the whole illness. Every time I eat, I seem to have to explain it to people.

Since this book is aimed at youth and teenagers, I would like to address an issue that I feel can occur frequently. This is when adults embarrass you in front of your peers. Maybe this doesn't happen to you, but it sure has happened to me. I categorize embarrassing adults into three categories: overconcerned, underconcerned, or not discrete.

If the adult is aware of your condition, they may ask how you are doing far too often. Every couple minutes, "Are you okay?" "How are you feeling?" "Are you sure you're feeling fine?" This can be embarrassing and irritating. It does show that they care, but can be hard to handle.

Secondly adults are sometimes ignorant and inconsiderate. They forget that you even have a disease and act inconsiderate towards your needs. They expect you to be like a normal kid. They don't realize you need to rest, and they expect you to be able to eat whatever a normal teenager would. I have had countless times where parents ask me, "Can't you eat this? It only has a little sugar."

When I say "I cannot eat any sugar" or "I can't eat any starches: no bread, pasta, or rice," they don't seem to understand. One woman tried to feed me chocolate syrup. You know, the kind they put on ice cream sundaes. I have no idea what was going through her mind. I can't eat sugar and she wants me to have chocolate syrup? She then proceeded to say that there wasn't that much sugar in it. And then went on further to explain how chocolate is good for you. Clearly this was ridiculous.

Lastly, some adults draw unwanted attention towards your problem, especially if they are unaware of it. A teacher once approached me when I was sitting at a dinner table with my classmates for a school event. I was not eating anything, and he noticed that. After coming up to me, he made a big fuss. "Why aren't you eating? Did you not get any food?" Now I realize there was no way he could have known, or ever would have been able to guess, that I had Crohn's disease. However the volume of his voice was unnecessary. This teacher later in the year would give out candy in class. When he noticed I wasn't eating it, he would comment on it even after I told him I couldn't eat sugar. Some people just really want you to eat what they're eating and they have a problem if you don't.

Of course not all adults will embarrass you. Since I went to a boarding school and could not bring my own food, the cooks made special meals for me based on my dietary restrictions. These adults made sure I always had what I needed to eat and allowed me to get my food without any questions. One particular cook had a family member on a similar diet. He was able to make me delicious meals every day at school. I am very grateful for adults who understand and never embarrass me.

On the other hand, parties in general can be a nightmare. What's worse than sitting around with food you can't eat, and hoping to escape conversation in time to make it to the bathroom?

Since I was diagnosed with Crohn's as an eight-year-old, I went to many birthday parties. If you are older, you probably won't be dealing with cake. You will be dealing with alcohol or other foods. Maybe you can drink alcohol and eat sugar and it doesn't affect you, but in my case sugar was the worst thing I could eat.

Here's a classic scenario of what I often experienced as a kid, and maybe you can relate. Imagine with me, if you will, that you've made it through the first hour or so of a birthday party just fine. Then someone brings the cake out. We all sing "Happy Birthday" and the cake is served.

"Do you want any cake?" I will get asked.

"No, thank you," I always politely refuse.

Then they always seem to ask again because people don't seem to take no for an answer. "Come on, just take a piece," they always insist.

After refusing a few times, you would imagine I'd get a break. But then I have to sit through the time when people are eating. During this time I pray to God that some kid won't ask me why I'm not eating cake. Once one kid asks, the other kids have their attention on me. And the conversation can either go two ways from there.

My first option is to be honest and tell them I can't eat sugar. That leads to the question, "Why?" Then once they find out I have a disease, it leads to a billion more questions. I have gotten questions like, "How did you get it?" "Is it contagious?" "What's it called?" I've even had the following question asked of me, "What happens if you eat sugar? Will you like explode or something?" I usually never take the option of being honest, since it is personal and not a desirable topic of conversation to talk about at a party.

The next option is to simply avoid the question or make up an excuse. You may simply state that you do not want any or are not hungry. This option leads to questions and seems to upset some people. "Why aren't you hungry?" "Everyone likes cake." And then the most famous and disliked, "Are you anorexic or something?" Normally girls will ask this.

I have been in many social situations that have been hard to get through and just flat-out embarrassing, and I'm sure you have had a few as well. But guess what? It will get easier for you to explain, or for you to handle ridicule. And the older you get, people grow up and mature, and aren't so concerned about what you're eating anymore. Junior high and high school years are most likely the worst, so just push through them. The best advice I could give you is to not worry so much about what other people think.

CHAPTER 6

NEWLY DIAGNOSED

When you are newly diagnosed, there are a few actions you should take. One of these will be finding information. Discover as much as you can about the disease! You're going to need to become organized.

Let's address how to find information. When asking questions or doing research, make sure you have reliable sources. When I was newly diagnosed, everyone I knew seemed to have advice they wished for me to try. Whether it was an herbal remedy, an actual medication, or an exercise, everyone thought they had a "cure." Still others said that if I went to their doctor I would be healed. Not everything everyone says will help you—in fact, it may even be harmful. Unless they have a degree in medicine, ask your specialist about what they are suggesting.

It is important to know which advice is good advice. This even comes into play when talking to your medical professional.

Doctors are human and make mistakes. They make their best educated guess, but with a disease as unpredictable as Crohn's sometimes it is hard to know what to do. If you're trying to make a hard decision, you may want to get a second opinion. Also you can do your own research online. It is great to have information from all different sources and then make a conclusion.

When you are newly diagnosed you need to get organized. Buy yourself a journal or a binder. Write down all your Crohn's symptoms every day. Maybe write down how many times you went to the bathroom that day. Write down your pain level. Make sure you take note of when you start or stop different medications. Write down if you tried a new food and monitor your symptoms the next few days. By writing everything down, you will be gathering vital information about yourself and your disease.

Keep your lab results and include them as well as other test results in the binder. If you compile all your test results and keep track of how you are feeling everyday, it will be much easier to figure out problems in the future. Since I was eight my mom took care of monitoring me. When I had a flare-up or a problem, she was able to look back and determine if it was a result of dietary change, medication, or something else.

~~~

"We can put her on a steroid. That should clear up the flare-up," my specialist assured us.

"If you look here on this date, you'll see she started having problems." My mom pointed at notes in her binder. "And then I wrote here that she started an antibiotic," my mother continued. "And after that her symptoms died down and her lab results were much better. So I think we should try that again."

"Yes, you could give that a try," the specialist agreed.

I sat in the seat watching them converse. Finally they decided they would give the antibiotic a try and I left the office feeling hopeful.

~~~

The scene above portrays the benefits of taking notes and getting to know your body. Learn what things affect you in what ways. Find out what works for you. My mom knew that an antibiotic helped me before, and so she was able to present that information to my doctor. I did end up using an antibiotic called Flagyl and it helped. Remember that your doctor has many patients and cannot possibly remember every detail about every one of them. If you record your symptoms and what has worked for you in the past, you can provide your doctor with this information when making a decision about a new medication.

Crohn's will alter your life. There are four ways in which most Crohn's patients' lives change. These differences are the food you eat, the need for a nearby restroom, the amount of energy you have, and medication.

First, let's talk about diet. Your doctor will give you some ideas on what to eat when you're first diagnosed. Most people agree that it is safe to stick with really bland, boring foods. Foods like bananas that are soft and easy to digest are great.

Other starchy items like bagels may be helpful to slow down the diarrhea.

After stabilizing somewhat, you might be able to try to introduce more foods into your diet. This has to be done very slowly and cautiously. You will need to decide if you are really in a place where you can afford to experiment with your diet. A rule of thumb should be to check with your physician.

Doctors may tell you that you can eat anything and that diet doesn't matter. This is because there is no certain link between food and Crohn's. No research proves that one food or another will make you sick. In fact it seems that everyone is different. There are certain things I know I can't eat or I will get sick, the main one being sugar. Yet other people can eat sugar, but get sick when they eat things I eat on a regular basis. Since the relationship between Crohn's disease and diet is not fully understood, doctors can't say for sure what to eat.

Despite this, I think most physicians and online sources agree on a few foods to stay away from. Often spicy food is something that should be avoided. Also nuts, popcorn, and seeds are banned. This makes sense considering they are sharp foods and can cause irritation to the intestines. Along with nuts and seeds, foods like celery and salads are hard to digest.

Depending on your dietary needs, you may have to bring food with you on the go. One product that I have discovered is freeze-dried fruit. It's a perfect snack. Eating at restaurants can be difficult. Because I have a limited diet, there is rarely anything on the menu that I can eat without placing a special order.

~~~

"She has Crohn's disease. She can't eat sesame seeds. So can we get two bottom buns on her hamburger?" my mom patiently explained. The waitress simply did not understand.

"Yes, but the bottom buns may have some sesame seeds on them," the waitress worried.

"That's okay if there are a few seeds on it; we can pick them off," my mom replied.

"Well, there are liability issues because the bottom bun may still have some seeds on them," the waitress stressed.

"She's not allergic; they are just rough and hard for her body to digest."

"I'm going to go get the manager, okay?" the waitress said.

I sighed. *I'm not allergic to nuts. I just can't eat sesame seeds! Is it that difficult to get two bottom buns on my hamburger?*

The manager approached us and my mom once again explained how I have Crohn's and can't digest the sesame seeds.

"But the buns have all been exposed to sesame seeds. It is a matter of liability, if she is allergic," the manager insisted.

"She isn't allergic," my dad pitched in, completely exasperated.

And this is why I hate eating out, I thought miserably.

~~~

Here is yet another story of a time when I had trouble ordering a burger. As you may well know, it is not good for Crohn's patients to eat red meat that is not fully cooked. It seems that many restaurants have a problem getting their burgers fully cooked . . .

~~~

I sat around the table with my family and looked hungrily at the burger I had ordered.

I started to eat my burger and was disturbed to see that the inside was red. Quickly, flagging the waitress down, we asked her if they could cook it further—it had to be *well done*. She brought it back to the kitchen.

After patiently waiting I received my burger for the second time. I was more than hungry. Before I put a piece into my mouth I realized the interior was still pink. Once again, the burger was brought back to the kitchen.

The food on my family's plate slowly disappeared. I looked down at my empty place on the table. *How hard is it to make sure a burger is thoroughly cooked?*

Finally, the waitress appeared and apologized profusely. I cut into my burger once again to find that it still looked the same. I sighed in frustration.

Seriously? You've got to be joking.

My parents looked at the burger and just shook their heads. "C'mon, Krystal, you can just eat at home."

~~~

As you can see, I have had my fair share of troubles when ordering burgers. Don't let these things get you down. Anywhere in life there will be miscommunication.

The second situation that's going to be different is the issue of needing a bathroom nearby at all times. Oftentimes when I went out places I became more familiar with the restroom at the place than the actual destination. Countless times at restaurants I spent almost as much time in the bathroom as I did at the table.

This can be an issue when you are traveling. If you have to spend a lot of time in the car, it might be hard for you. Try to familiarize yourself with exits on the highway before you go anywhere. Make sure you can find somewhere to stop and use the restroom. And it is probably a good idea to bring a change of clothes if the diarrhea is out of control.

And try not to get too discouraged. The disease will get better, and the diarrhea will be less severe. And eventually you may reach remission. In the meantime, you're not alone. All of us Crohn's patients worry about finding a bathroom in time. Some of us have even had accidents on more than one occasion.

~~~

"Um, Dad, where are we going?" I nervously asked.

He answered me, but I wasn't listening. What I really wanted to know was not *where* we were going, but how *long* it would take to get there.

". . . it will only take twenty minutes or so," he finished replying.

My ears perked up when he said "twenty minutes." That's not a bad drive for someone without Crohn's. But I worried. Would I be able to make it without any accidents?

I sat in the car while we drove off. Looking out the window, I was extremely tense. Counting the seconds, I hoped that the urge to use the restroom wouldn't overtake me. But the urge started to come.

Immediately my eyes scanned the freeway for the nearest off-ramp. "How soon can we make it to the bathroom?" I asked.

My parents knew what this meant and got off the road as soon as possible. In case you were wondering, I did make it to the bathroom in time.

~~~

The third aspect that will change in your life is the amount of energy you have. Fatigue affects Crohn's patients because they aren't getting the nutrients they need. Sleep has been crucial for me, especially during the thick of my flare-ups. I do really well when I get ten hours of sleep. The weeks of school where I am only getting five or six hours of sleep at night, I start getting run down.

If you need to make some lifestyle changes, do it. Cut out some activities or sports if you have to. Above all else, take care of your body and make sure you're getting enough rest.

During my childhood my family and another family made an annual trip to San Diego for the Fourth of July. It was always a lot of fun. For hours we walked up and down the streets acting like tourists. After I got Crohn's though, the trip was different.

It was hard for me to keep up. The rest of my family and their family had no problem walking all around, but I got very tired out. Not only was I tired, but I had to use the restroom more often than before I was diagnosed. Additionally, it was hard to find places to eat.

I remember, after walking all day, we went back to the hotel at night to swim. I was physically drained and I just couldn't swim. Years prior, I would have had no problem keeping up with all the activities. Now it was different though. I sat and watched the other kids splash in the pool.

But don't let this story depress you. I have built up my health over the years and have reached remission. I am no longer tired easily and I can handle great amounts of strain and activity. Just take care of your body, and your strength will improve too!

Lastly, medication will be an issue. Before you had Crohn's, chances are the only pills you took were daily multivitamins. Everything changes, as I'm sure you've realized. It is probable you may have to take medications at different times of day. This means you'll have to remember when to take them, and you'll have to bring them with you if you plan on going out. Buy yourself some sort of small backpack or a purse to bring your medications in. If you're wearing pants, you can put the pills in a Ziploc bag and just slip the bag in your pocket. Whatever works for you is fine.

When you begin taking medication it may seem weird, but soon you won't even think twice about it. It becomes part of your daily routine. If you feel embarrassed about taking pills in public, never fear! There are always places you can go to get away from prying eyes. I remember having to take pills in between classes at school.

~~~

The teacher was explaining an important concept to the class. My eyes weren't focused on her though; they were fixed on the clock above her head. It was time for my next dose of medicine. I eyed my classmates to see if anyone was looking.

No one was looking at me for the time being, but I knew taking pills in school would draw attention to me. I decided it wasn't worth the risk. So I raised my hand.

"Yes. Krystal?" The teacher wondered why I had interrupted her.

"Um, may I please go to the restroom?" I asked. She was aware of my condition and so she let me go.

With my pills in my pocket, I quickly exited the room and went to the bathroom. The halls were relatively empty and I took my dose at the drinking fountain before heading back to class.

~~~

On more than one occasion I took my water bottle and pills and hid in a bathroom stall to take them. So if you're out in public and you don't want any questions, just head to the bathroom. Of course you could always just say that its allergy medication or something of the sort. The important thing is not to miss a dose because you're out and about.

These are just a few ways your life will change. There are many other differences you might notice. However, these are the most obvious and prominent changes that can occur.

CHAPTER 7

THE DOCTOR'S OFFICE AND THE LAB: HOMES AWAY FROM HOME

Trips to the doctors will become a regular part of your life, until you reach remission. During flare-ups it seemed almost every few days I was in and out of the doctor's office. I spent hours sitting in lobbies staring at colored paintings on the walls and listening to sick children cough and cry. I've heard hundreds of nurses call my name, awakening me from my wandering thoughts.

There are many different types of doctors. I visited several specialists and I also had a general doctor. Each specialist was different. There was one in particular who was far different from the others. Seeing her was not an average experience since she had a team of specialists. What I mean by that is, in the beginning of the visit, the nutritionists would come in. They spent around twenty minutes with my family and I talking all about

71

diet. Then a group of counselors would come in. After some time the doctor would finally arrive. Still afterwards usually nurses would come in to take my blood.

Location will also vary. My general doctor was about twenty minutes away, while one of my pediatric gastroenterologists was several hours away. When you have to travel hours away it can be draining, but it is worth it when you get help. Don't just go to the clinic across the street from your house for the sake of convenience. Crohn's is a complicated disease and it is best to have doctors who specialize in IBD or gastroenterology.

Many life-altering decisions are made in doctor's offices. After some visits I felt discouraged, while still others gave me a glimmer of hope. So which doctor should you choose, and how do you find one? I found mine by word of mouth. Think if you know anyone else with IBD or some kind of gastrointestinal problems. Ask them who they see. You can research online to find out where medical clinics are located. Your general doctor will also be able to recommend a specialist to you within their medical group.

If you are going to see multiple doctors, it will be crucial to have cooperation. All three of my doctors were acquainted with each other. And we made sure to consult the other two when one of them wanted to change something. Sometimes they disagreed, but we were always able to come to a conclusion on what seemed best. You and your doctors are a team. Work together with them and make sure everyone involved is informed and on the same page.

Make the most of your visits. Come up with questions to ask, and take part in the discussion. Learn as much about your disease from them as you can. Don't just rely on everything your doctor says; provide some of your own input. Research different treatments online and discuss which ones you'd like to try and why. Then ask them what they think about that.

When I was younger I was afraid of doctor's offices and doctors themselves. I hope you don't make that mistake. Now that I am older I am not afraid at all. I trust my specialist and try to work with her to keep my Crohn's at bay. They know more about the disease than you do, but you know more about your body. They rely on you to tell them how you feel and how you're doing. And you rely on them to figure out what's wrong. Don't leave it all to them, yet don't try to do it all yourself. Once more, work as a team!

A simple task you can do is to understand your lab results. This way you aren't counting on your doctor to tell you how you are doing. You can both receive the results and know from the numbers what condition you are in. If you don't receive a copy of your lab results, request that they be faxed to you. After understanding what your labs mean, you may see why your doctor wants to try a specific route of treatment. As I said earlier, learn a lot and be inquisitive.

While I don't understand everything on my lab slip, there are always two numbers I look at. The first is my sed rate, or sedimentation rate. It may be shown on your lab as ESR, which stands for erythrocyte sedimentation rate. The sedimentation rate measures inflammation. The way that the sed rate is measured is by the amount of red blood cells that settle on the bottom of a blood vial in an hour. The more cells there are at the bottom, the more inflammation there is. This is because when there is inflammation in the body certain proteins cause the red blood cells to stick together and fall more quickly. A sedimentation rate is measured in mm per hour. For men the normal range is 0–15 mm/hr and for women it is 0–20mm/hr. The lower the sed rate the better! Now that I am in remission my number is always somewhere between an eight and a ten. The ESR rate doesn't always show all the inflammation though.

So the other number you can look for on your lab results is the CRP, or C-reactive protein test. A CRP test measures the amount of C-reactive protein in your blood, which basically measures the amount of inflammation. The normal range for the CRP is 0–1.0 mg/dL. So anything above a one on your lab results could mean inflammation even if your ESR rate is low.

Speaking about lab test results, now let's talk about the actual laboratory. This is the place where you will be getting your blood drawn. Visiting this place became a regular habit. For six months I used to have to go once a week. I got to know the lab very well. I was a nervous wreck at first. The nervous feeling lasted for a year or maybe even two. I think that was mostly because I was so young. Now I hardly get nervous at all. I just want to get it over with as quickly as possible and move on with my day. Who wants to spend any more time than necessary in that place? Not me.

I remember when I was younger I used to get rewarded for getting my blood taken. I would get to go to the toy store. That honestly was great for me when I was little, but as you get older you don't want toys anymore.

After a while, you just have to do it because you know it's best. There are a few things you can do to make it easier. If you have large veins, getting your blood taken is probably not that big of an issue. I, on the other hand, have small veins. If you are like me here are some ideas that can help.

Drink water. By drinking water I don't mean sip on water. I mean drink water to the point where you feel like you might explode. Alright, so perhaps that's a little excessive, but you get the picture. Not only will it help you to not feel faint, but it will help to enlarge your veins. Some blood tests require fasting beforehand, but if yours doesn't then eat something too. It will help you feel stronger in general and not as faint. If getting your blood taken is truly a pain, treat yourself afterwards. Reward yourself with a favorite food to eat or a fun activity.

After going to the same lab for a year or so, the people there become familiar. You may start to have a preference for who you like to have take your blood. When I was little there was only one man who could get my vein the first time. I would only go to him. When I got older my vein was easier to get and I let anyone who was available do it. Nevertheless, I still had my preferences.

~~~

Inwardly I groaned. *Oh no,* I thought. The dark-haired woman called my name and told me to sit down. *Not her again,* I complained in my head.

"Which arm would you like?" she asked as usual.

"I don't care," I replied hoping that she would feel more favorable towards me if I let her pick.

She picked the left arm, as usual.

"Make a fist," she said with her face expressionless. I did as I was told.

Poking around she searched for the vein on my left arm that always seemed to evade her. She continued on anyway and pulled out a blue elastic strip of rubber from the drawer. When she tied it around my upper arm I flinched.

My eyes widened as I looked at my arm. The blue elastic was tied so tightly it looked as if it would sever my arm into two pieces. Squirming in my chair I wondered why on earth she insisted on making it that unnecessarily tight. No one else I had ever had tied it that tight.

Now it was time for the rubbing alcohol. She rubbed it on my arm. Frantically I blew on it trying to dry it. But she liked to pierce me as soon as she put it on. It always stung like crazy.

I blew and blew and blew, but I wasn't quick enough. In went the needle.

My sneaky left vein rolled away like it always did.

"It keeps moving," she complained as if it wasn't usual.

Of course it does, I thought irritated. *Yet you still always choose the left arm.*

~~~

What can I say? Everyone has their quirks I suppose.

So far I've discussed a little bit about the doctor's office and the laboratory. There is a chance that you're not quite as familiar with either of those places. And chances are you aren't excited about them becoming your "homes away from home" as I've titled this chapter.

When I was younger I started to wonder if this was what my life would be like. I wondered if I would ever have a social life again, or if the only socializing I would do would be with lab technicians. During flare-ups I was in and out of the medical facilities all the time. But you will have times in your life where the Crohn's is less active and won't require as many trips to the doctors or the lab. Until then keep in mind these visits are all part of the journey to health.

CHAPTER 8

CROHN'S AND
PHYSICAL APPEARANCE

This chapter really only applies to youth who aren't fully developed yet. Crohn's disease can prevent growth. The reason for this is mostly due to malnutrition. If you think about your body, you realize you need energy. If your intestines are damaged and unable to take in nutrients, how can you mature? In addition the steroids used to treat the disease also stunt growth.

Before Crohn's I was always a step ahead of my peer group. I was inches taller than most of my peers in preschool, and the doctors determined I would be tall. When I was diagnosed with Crohn's in third grade, my growing slowed down drastically.

In junior high school especially, when you are trying to fit in, this can be extremely difficult. I cannot tell you how many shocked expressions I received from people who thought I was younger than I actually was. A major motivation for wanting to get into remission is simply so I could grow.

~~~

The water was splashing up upon the sand. I was at work building a sandcastle with my friend and her boyfriend. Presently he spoke up about my size.

"You're just so tiny," he chuckled.

"I'm only a couple years younger than you!" I protested.

"Yeah but still, look at your arms. They're like sticks," he argued back.

I looked down at my thin arms that were crossed across my chest in an act of defiance.

"It's not even normal," he laughed joking around with me.

I was left standing there without a comeback, because he was more right than he knew. He wasn't even aware I had Crohn's.

"Whatever," I huffed wishing I was bigger.

~~~

Being small was really frustrating for me, especially in the junior high years. Not only were my friends getting taller, but they were looking older. My female friends' faces and bodies were changing shape, and my guy friends were getting deeper voices. And still I looked pretty much the same.

So what can you do? Truly there isn't much you can do. The two factors affecting your growth are steroids and Crohn's. You have to be on steroids oftentimes, though, to control the Crohn's. Once the disease is under control you can wean off the steroids. This will significantly improve your growth!

~~~

"Last time I saw you a few months ago you had just gotten off the steroid you were on. Is that correct?" The doctor observed, looking at her notes.

I smiled and nodded my head eagerly.

"Well, let's check your height then."

Hopping off the table I stood by the wall where the tape measure was. I expected the usual 5' ¼" result. *I can't remember a time when I wasn't 5' ¼"*.

"You're 5' 1"," she stated.

I went and sat back down.

"Wait, what?" Finally processing what she had just said, I immediately rejoiced. "I grew three-quarters of an inch and it's only been a few months!"

My smile was as wide as it could be.

~~~

Try to eat really healthy nutritious food. And get plenty of sleep. Sleep is important for teens even without Crohn's. During times when I was the most sick, I often slept at least twelve hours. Depending on your work or school schedule I realize this might not be possible for you, but try to get as much sleep as you can.

Crohn's probably won't affect your appearance very much. However there are a few ways in which it might. Crohn's patients are thin and often look emaciated. Because of this their peers occasionally think they are anorexic, especially if they are girls.

Weight cannot be maintained because of frequent diarrhea and damaged bowels. The intestines have a hard time thoroughly digesting food. Since the food isn't digested, it is hard for a Crohn's patient to put on any weight at all.

During the hardest parts of my journey with Crohn's, I was eating up to five meals a day. There was a certain point after one of my periods of remission where I fell back into a relapse. I was losing more and more weight. My parents started getting concerned and they realized that my Crohn's had come back.

My parents finally wouldn't allow me to do many activities unless I weighed a certain amount. I would consume large amounts of water before stepping on the scale in the hope that I would be heavier. Regardless, I could hardly maintain my weight of about sixty pounds.

It honestly is horrifying to see your weight drop continually day after day. No matter how much you eat, it is extremely challenging to just maintain your weight. There came a point where I realized that if I stopped consuming large amounts of food, I could become fatally thin. This was frightening, but I have made it through! Now I can even afford to exercise and lose a few pounds, even though I am still thin. I am no longer sickly thin.

Moving on, another physical attribute that I had when I was really sick was a pale complexion. This was a more noticeable thing for me, being Irish and German. If you are of another nationality the pale factor might not affect your appearance much. Probably all Crohn's patients grow more pale when they are really sick. Just the fact that we lose so much blood and water from diarrhea makes us more fatigued and pale.

Medications can also alter your appearance. Prednisone was really the only medication I took that changed my appearance, so that is what I will be talking about. I already discussed prednisone's side effects, but I wanted to focus on the physical attributes it creates.

Firstly prednisone causes the "chipmunk cheeks." This is probably the hardest side effect to deal with as far as appearance goes. You can go from having a slender face one day to a completely round face the next day.

~~~

Zipping up the velvet purple dress I stole a glance in the mirror. My eyes traveled up my thin legs all the way to my face. My face was round. My cheeks were large. I didn't recognize myself. I came downstairs to leave the house for a church event.

My mom snapped a picture of me with my brother.

"Smile!" she said.

As the flash went off I couldn't stop thinking about my face. Would I ever look the same again?

~~~

Yes, you will look the same again! Once you are off prednisone or whatever steroid you're on, the effects will go away.

Unfortunately, along with the round face, prednisone can cause acne. My acne really increased while I was taking prednisone. Again, don't worry; it should clear up after you stop the medication. Meanwhile wash your face with cleansers and if it gets uncontrollable find medication for it.

Other than that, Crohn's patients normally don't look too different on the outside. Usually they are very skinny, but otherwise normal looking. The hardest issue for me as a preteen and a teenager was being small. It made me feel shy in social groups. Many times I would be asked how old I was.

~~~

"Yeah, okay. You're how old? Like twelve?" the boys at the skate park laughed.

My mouth hung open. *Did I really look that young?* "Twelve? I'll bet I'm older than you," I retorted angrily.

"I doubt it," another boy taunted.

"I'm fourteen!" I insisted.

This time their mouths hung open.

"Hey you!" a guy yelled to another, "How old does this girl look?"

"Maybe thirteen . . . maybe twelve . . . or eleven . . . hard to say," he replied.

"She's fourteen. Can you believe it?" he stated.

I was embarrassed that these kids who were younger than I couldn't believe how old I was.

~~~

Because of multiple scenarios like this, I felt insecure and scared. Feelings of insignificance and inferiority filled me. I undermined my value because of my appearance and what others thought. Truthfully, it really didn't matter what those silly boys at the skate park thought. No matter how young I looked, I was still me. The same goes for you as well. Know who you are and looks won't define you. There's one last flashback I'd like to share with you that occurred about a week ago. Keep in mind that now my Crohn's is in remission.

~~~

I walked into the doctor's office for my appointment. The nurse ushered me into a small room to check my vitals. She noticed my mom in the doorway. "Why is your mom here?" she asked.

I was a little confused. "She drove me," I answered.

Now the nurse looked equally confused. "How old are you?" she asked.

"Sixteen," I replied.

"Oh wow!" She looked taken aback.

"How old did you think I was?" I wondered.

"At least twenty-two or so," she responded, much to my delight.

~~~

It's funny how life turns out. No longer do people think I am younger, but older. Often as a freshman in high school I was asked if I was a freshman in college. Whenever you feel dismayed, remember there is a lot of hope! Focus on getting the disease under control and you will grow just as I did.

CHAPTER 9

THE AFTERMATH OF CROHN'S AND REBUILDING

Even long after your symptoms have gone away, emotional scars of the disease remain. There are many ways in which the disease can change your personality. Sometimes the emotional effects of the disease seem more devastating than the physical ones. How can you recover from the trauma of dealing with Crohn's, especially as a young person?

Let's discuss some ways in which Crohn's affects you. It's easy to feel misunderstood when you have Crohn's. It's a pretty personal disease and isn't something you want to be really open about. I mean, who wants to talk about how many times they went to the bathroom that day? With this being said, it is easy to become isolated and feel alone. No matter how many times I've tried to explain what I'm going through, no one could understand. It's one of those things you have to experience.

Sometimes I feel so lonely. My friends don't have a clue what my disease is or how it affects me. And I don't really want to go into details with them either. My family has tried to understand but it's sometimes difficult for them as well.

As a result of feeling so isolated, I began to separate myself from people. I knew they wouldn't understand and if I tried to explain I'd get grossed-out reactions or embarrassing questions. I felt different from other peers. Even little comments in social groups reminded me that I wasn't "normal."

~~~

The health teacher asked the class, "Are all of you relatively healthy teenagers? Raise your hands."

Students raised their hands absentmindedly. They were bored with the question and didn't have to think twice to answer it. I looked around the classroom at all the hands and slowly raised mine as well.

The voice of the teacher faded as I became lost in my thoughts. Thoughts of sadness and even thoughts of jealousy of the other students' health popped up in my mind.

What would it be like to be perfectly healthy? What if my only health concerns were the flu or a cold? What if the only medicine I needed was cough syrup? I tried to remember what it was like before Crohn's. I imagined my doctor's file being small; I also imagined being able to eat whatever I wanted whenever I wanted.

~~~

Crohn's can create a feeling of loneliness and isolation. It can also mold your personality in other ways. After the disease took its course I began to be more controlling. The most unfortunate aspect about having Crohn's is you have no say in what goes on in your body. At any time the relentless disease can strike. At any moment it can return with full force and fury. This is a fact that certainly can be hard to face and accept. Because of the unpredictable nature of the disease, I have become very resistant to any change in my life. I am not as flexible of a person as I used to be.

In addition, I have become more afraid. The disease initiated a constant feeling of fear. This pattern has continued even though I am in remission. It started with fear of needles, then it moved to a fear of treatments and the disease itself. After that it was the thought of relapse that scared me. Then I began to become anxious about things that had no connection with Crohn's.

Today I felt a pang of pain in my side. Immediately terror gripped my heart. A million thoughts went through my mind. *Oh no, the Crohn's is back. I need to get some blood work done. Maybe I should get scoped; I haven't been scoped in a couple years. I wonder how bad it is. What am I going to do? Maybe I can get away with just taking an antibiotic.* Then I realized stress is only going to make things worse and I proceeded to try and calm myself down.

Next, I want to talk to you about memories. Even long after certain events have happened, the memories remain. The hospital was a sore topic for me for years, and it still is. I have been inside a hospital building only a few times since I was admitted.

The first time was to visit a neighbor who had been injured shortly after I was diagnosed. It was very hard for me to visit the same hospital I had once been in. I focused on our neighbor. It wasn't until I was out in the parking lot walking to our car that I broke down. I began to feel panicked and started to cry.

Even recently, years after the experience, I once again visited a hospital and started to feel a little panicky. It wasn't even the hospital I had been in before, but it was a hospital nevertheless. One of my brother's friends had been admitted overnight. We came to visit him.

~~~

As I stood in the room, all of the chatter faded. I wasn't paying attention to what the mothers were talking about or what my brother was saying or even the boy himself.

My eyes were scanning the room. They moved over the bed. It was a classic hospital bed similar to mine. It was electric and you could adjust it as needed. Then I spotted the TV and of course the cards and the flowers.

My thoughts flashed back to my hospital room. There were so many stuffed animals and the nurse was irritated because the environment was no longer sterile. I remembered all the gifts, cards, and "Get Well" balloons. Of course none of them could heal me.

I was brought back to the present as I continued to look around this boy's room. My eyes wandered to the IV machine. There was the bag dripping fluid. *Drip, drip, drip.* The fluid fell from a plastic bag hanging from the machine. I watched as it traveled down through the tube towards the needle lodged in the boy's arm.

This brought back memories of my own visit. I remembered the nurse who struggled to get the needle in my arm. I remembered my fright of needles after that. Memories of the PICC line came back and tears stung my eyes.

Suddenly I felt overwhelmed being in the room and just wanted to get out. As my brother and the boy were talking, and my parents and his were chatting, I was lost in my own little world. It was a world filled with memories I wished I could forget.

~~~

In this chapter I've just discussed feeling alone and different, becoming controlling, being afraid, and living with memories. So what can you do about these difficulties? I'll address them in order.

Firstly, feeling abnormal is actually really hard to deal with sometimes. You've probably heard things along the lines of "that's what makes you special" or "you're a unique individual." These are all true. One of the wisest comments I've heard is "God knew you could handle this. You are a strong individual." It makes me feel better to hear this. It's true. Most kids could not handle half the hardships we, as Crohn's patients, have to go through.

You aren't the only one out there who feels alone or misunderstood. Get connected. Find other peers with Crohn's. Ask your doctor about support groups. Research online. There are many bloggers and YouTube channels that you can access as well. You might feel like you aren't normal when you're at school, but when you're in a group of people that is going through the same circumstances as you, you'll probably feel right at home. Looking back, I wish that I would have done this. And even though I'm in remission now, I think I may try a Crohn's support group.

Secondly, when conquering controlling personality traits you may have developed, take the same approach as with the fear. Face yourself and force yourself to be more flexible. You might not like change but force yourself to accept it. Maybe even take a leap and try something new every once in a while! Try to become more relaxed and less uptight. When a new idea is suggested, stay open to it. When life doesn't go the way you planned, take a deep breath and just go with it.

Thirdly, conquering any fearful personality traits requires effort. To put it simply, face your fears and step outside your comfort zone. Face what you're afraid of, whether it's a high sedimentation rate on your lab results or a horrible surgery. We've all gone through hard situations like these, and I'm sure we wouldn't like to again.

Going through a flare a second, third, or even fourth time seems as hard as the first, but it's a little less scary. If you made it through previous flare-ups, you can make it through this one. Crohn's is a challenge, but it helps you to become a stronger person. Don't let Crohn's defeat you!

There was one treatment that I was frightened to try. That was Remicade. First of all I hate needles, second I hate hospitals, and third I hate medication. Besides all that, Remicade was a relatively new drug on the market with warnings of dangerous complications. I finally decided that I would do it if it was the best option for me.

I never actually had to take Remicade after all, but it was important for me to be willing to do whatever the doctors thought was best. Just the fact that I faced my fear and was willing to do whatever it took gave me a feeling of strength.

The key is to overcome the fear and be victorious. Don't let anything conquer you or get in the way of living your life. You can have a great life; in fact I'd even say it's possible to have an even better life after getting Crohn's than before you had it. You may not believe me—especially if you are in the middle of a flare-up—but it is true.

One factor to think about when you face hardships is that you're only becoming stronger. Things normal teenagers are scared to death to do are so insignificant for me. When I hear teenagers worrying about normal everyday problems, I just chuckle to myself. I can easily handle their petty problems. Because of this, people look up to me as a strong person who can handle difficulties well. And they will look up to you too.

Fourthly, when dealing with bad memories, it is important to talk to people you can confide in. You can do it! Make sure you have a safe environment that you can talk in and not be overheard. Also make sure you have a person whom you can really trust. If you don't feel like you have a parent or a family member you can really trust, find out about counseling. Or if you feel comfortable talking about it with peers, ask your doctor about support groups as I mentioned before. And try not to dwell on the past; look ahead and find hope in the future. Healing will come, emotionally and physically.

Perhaps you don't believe in God, but there is a quote that stuck out to me this morning that I'd like to share. It says that

God is strong in your weakness. I believe that God works stronger in my life during times when I am weak. When I can't do it on my own, He takes over.

One specific time I was really desperate. I don't even remember exactly why I was so despairing. I was just overwhelmed with grief and hopelessness. I lay on the floor crumpled up and sobbed. I sobbed and sobbed for all I was worth. Then I cried out to God.

I needed something to cling to, anything at all. I needed a sign. After crying and praying, I opened up the Bible. The passage I read was about the disciples receiving the Holy Spirit and power from God. And it went on to say that after they received it the place where they were was shaken.

Immediately after reading that there was an earthquake. That was just the sign I needed. God was with me, and I could do this.

It's very possible you don't believe in religion or any higher power; however I just wanted to put that out there since it was a life-altering moment. I was about to give up, but then I caught sight of hope and got back up on my feet.

After giving a lot of thought to the emotional effects Crohn's has had on me, I see a pattern. Perhaps I'm wrong, but this is what happened to me. I hope you can identify with it.

When I was diagnosed with Crohn's, I cut out extra activities from my life, obviously since I was very sick. But then I isolated further. I stopped keeping in contact with many acquaintances. No longer did I talk to my neighbors or people in my community. From there I stopped talking to some people at school who I didn't know very well. I no longer went to church events and only attended on Sundays. I even started losing connection with close friends.

The pattern is like an onion. Slowly all the layers are peeled off until nothing is left. Severe sickness can cause the layers to peel away, but once you are better it is important to build the levels back. Rebuild your life. If you see that this pattern is or was true for yourself, stop it if you can. If you have already isolated from activities, friends, and family, it's time to rebuild!

Open up to your family again and reconnect with your best friends. Don't allow yourself to end up alone. After you've crossed those bridges, start talking to other people at school or work. Then talk to acquaintances in your community. Say hi to your neighbors again. Don't let Crohn's cause you to withdraw from society! Get your life back. Start old activities again. Join groups and meet people. You can have success. I hope this chapter has given you some helpful ideas on repairing the damage Crohn's can do to your social life, personality, and memories.

CHAPTER 10

SCD DIET

I talked about how to repair some of the emotional damage Crohn's can do in the last chapter. Now I want to introduce the diet that was able to bring me back to health. Although it is a long process to start the diet, it may be your ticket to health. I recommend asking your gastroenterologist about it before you start. The website for the diet is breakingtheviciouscycle.com. The following paragraph is from the website under the "About the Diet" tab:

The allowed carbohydrates are monosaccharaides and have a single molecule structure that allows them to be easily absorbed by the intestine wall. Complex carbohydrates which are disaccharides (double molecules) and polysaccharides (chain molecules) are not allowed. Complex carbohydrates that are not easily digested feed harmful bacteria in our intestines causing them to overgrow producing byproducts and inflaming the intestine wall. The diet works by starving out these bacteria and restoring the balance of bacteria in our gut.

So the idea is all complex carbohydrates are taken out of your diet in order to starve out the bad bacteria. The diet essentially consists of meat, vegetables, fruits, and some dairy such as butter and certain cheeses.

This SCD diet certainly is strict. Strict may be an understatement. It does not allow processed food and sugar is forbidden. Also no bread, pasta, rice, or potatoes are allowed. Simple carbs like fruits are fine.

Like most diets it definitely requires a lot of self-control and discipline, but is worth it! I've been on the SCD diet for three years now and haven't had any symptoms. My labs haven't shown any indication of inflammation either. Additionally, just a week ago I was scoped and the results were amazing.

The official book for information on it is called *Breaking the Vicious Cycle*. The author of the book is Elaine Gottschall. Elaine was a normal mother until one of her two daughters became violently ill with Ulcerative Colitis. The disease was debilitating and none of the medications did the trick. Her daughter was slipping towards death and Elaine became desperate. She finally met with a ninety-two-year-old doctor, Dr. Haas. He had been working on the diet, despite the criticism from other doctors who didn't believe it was important.

Elaine's daughter tried these foods and was successful. Her symptoms improved in a few months and she started to grow again. Within two years she was free from all symptoms. Elaine wanted others to know about the SCD diet and so she learned as much as she could and earned degrees in biology, nutritional biochemistry, and cellular biology. Furthermore she proceeded to write a book.

The book, *Breaking the Vicious Cycle*, clearly demonstrates the correct way to start this diet. I highly recommend reading the book thoroughly as well as talking to your doctor before you begin. The book includes a list of legal/illegal foods and also explains the process of slowly introducing new foods.

When I first heard about the SCD diet, I was amazed. As I scrolled through the list of illegal foods on the website, the longer I looked, the more I was astonished. All the foods I was accustomed to eating were on the illegal list. Previously, I had been on a diet that revolved around bland starchy food, and now I was about to cut that out completely.

In the beginning I really did not want to try this diet. My parents wanted me to begin this new diet but I was horrified at the thought of giving up all delicious unhealthy treats. Finally, I decided being sick was worse than living without certain foods. I was still reluctant and only halfheartedly tried these new foods.

I started off by consuming fewer carbohydrates, but hadn't cut them out of my diet completely. Once I was at Subway and I ordered a sandwich, then I realized I couldn't eat the bread. *What is a sandwich without bread?* I had wondered to myself.

Eventually though I decided to really try it without cutting corners. It was difficult to adjust to this drastic diet. Initially I barely ate anything for about two weeks.

I ate homemade chicken broth for the majority of the day. This can easily be made by soaking a whole chicken in a large pot. In addition, I ate homemade applesauce. You can make it in a slow cooker as well. Later on I discovered that you can buy applesauce without sugar in it. If I had known this earlier, it would have saved a lot of time.

Another part of my diet was jello, but not the kind sold in most stores. Remember, processed foods and sugars are illegal on the diet. The jello has to be homemade too. You may be reading this thinking, *There is no way I'm going on this diet.* Those same thoughts ran through my head. Now I consider it as one of the best choices I have ever made. Getting back to the jello, Welches 100% pure white grape juice has been my best friend on this diet. This is because there is no added sugar and it tastes amazing. Just add gelatin and you have yourself some all-natural jello.

Once I decided to not mess around and really follow all the directions, my symptoms did not get better right away. In fact they got worse. All I could think about was delicious creamy pasta, or a nice loaf of bread with melted butter. Carbohydrates were on my mind and I continually craved them.

Not only did I crave carbs, but my condition worsened a little. This was to be expected. The goal of the diet is to starve off bad bacteria, which feed off sugar and carbs. When you start the diet those bacteria die off and you might feel a little lousy. But if you get through this short phase, you'll be glad you did.

This brings up another point. Don't try this diet out in the middle of the school year. I recommend starting in the summer or when you're on a break from school. It takes a while to get used to and you will need a lot of rest and time to adjust.

After the second week I got really sick. I vomited all night and I felt as if all the life had been sucked out of me. The next morning I lay on the couch pondering what to do.

~~~

What else can I do? I really thought this was going to work. I don't want to have to take drugs. But I'm only getting worse, and the only treatment left is Remicade.

"Krystal, I think maybe you should stop. You gave the diet a try." My dad looked at me with sympathetic eyes.

"You don't have to do this; you can just stop right this very minute," my mom added.

"I don't know what to do," I voiced bewilderedly. It was the honest truth. I had no idea where to go from here.

With determination I finally spoke. "I've gone this far. There's no turning back now."

~~~

Over the next couple weeks I got better. I never threw up again, and I felt stronger. The diet was very bland and it was scarcely any food, but everything was going okay. I stuck with it and as the months passed I added more and more foods. I bought a few SCD cookbooks and learned how to make some pretty decent-tasting recipes.

This diet is a challenge, but it has been well worth it for me. I have been symptom free for about four years now. No one can tell that I have Crohn's. People only ask questions when I eat my weird, yet healthy food. But I don't ever have to run off to the bathroom or be doubled over in pain anymore. I feel strong and invigorated.

I think the most challenging part of the diet was figuring out what I could eat. Everything seems to have sugar in it.

~~~

My eyes wandered to the packaged meat in the refrigerated section of the grocery store. Picking up a packet of sliced turkey lunch meat, I placed it in the cart.

"Are you sure there's no sugar in it?" my dad asked.

"Dad, it's turkey. It's not sweetened," I stated. Just to make sure I checked the ingredients list. *Sugar.* There it was: that awful ingredient that seemed to be in everything.

"Try this one." My dad picked an organic healthier brand off the shelf. I looked at the ingredients. *Evaporated Cane Juice.*

"Evaporated cane juice? Really? Nice way to try to make sugar sound healthier," I groaned in frustration.

"We'll have to try and find another store," my dad concluded.

~~~

In addition to foods like lunch meat, almost all juices have added sugar as well. Most may claim they don't, but often times they contain a small amount from juice concentrate. After checking labels I came to realize it is very difficult to find foods that haven't been sweetened.

But it can be done! You just have to look diligently and be persistent. I have found certain health food stores like Whole Foods carry turkey lunch meat without sugar at their deli. I also found freeze-dried fruit with no additives. You will have to be creative, but I know you can do it!

One last and very important thing you should know about the SCD diet is that it is not a regular course of treatment. Your doctor won't mention it to you. In the medication chapter I discussed the usual treatment options there are. Those are well researched and widely accepted throughout the medical community. One or more of these accepted medications will be recommended to you.

Follow your doctor's recommended treatment, and then ask about the diet. If your doctor thinks that it's a good idea to try it then do it. Remember to keep going with your prescriptions. The SCD diet is NOT a substitute for your medication. When I started I stayed on my maintenance medication.

Going off medication and relying solely on the SCD diet could be a dangerous move. It is so easy to slip up with the diet, and if you aren't on any other medication you won't have anything to fall back on. I strongly suggest you don't try to get off your medications at least until you're older. That way you won't have to worry about relapsing and having to take steroids, which might stop your growth.

CHAPTER 11

SELF-CONTROL

The hardest part of the SCD diet, or any diet, is simply having the discipline and self-control to follow through with it. It is easy to lose self-control especially after your health begins to improve. I find myself in a cycle that maybe you can relate with.

When I first was diagnosed in 2005 I was critically ill. For the next two years it was a rocky road. My lab reports were inconsistent; some were really bad and some were better. Never was I really stable. After all the ups and downs, around the year 2007, my condition worsened. The Crohn's was out of control.

I had been taking almost all the drugs available to treat Crohn's except for Remicade. This was something I really did not want to have to take. My doctor called to let us know we needed to act, and that we needed to do it fast. He informed my mom that he was putting in a request to get me into the emergency room. Let's just say I really did not want to go.

That evening I vomited all night and into the morning. For seventeen hours straight, I was kneeling on the hard bathroom floor wishing this would end. However, an extraordinary event took place.

~~~

When the light of morning came, I suddenly felt well. Despite not having gotten any sleep, I got up and wandered downstairs.

The house was empty, and so weakly I went out to the backyard. One of my friends from school was swimming in the pool. My mom turned around and saw me in the doorway.

"Krystal, how are you feeling?" She came over to me concerned.

"I feel okay," I said, realizing the nausea was gone.

I wobbled a little bit and so she helped me over to the water's edge.

"Are you hungry?" my mom asked.

"She's making pizza!" my classmate shouted from the pool.

I looked at my mom and asked, "Can I please try some? I feel perfectly fine."

Pretty soon I was eating pizza and swimming in the pool like nothing had ever happened.

~~~

My mom called the specialist and told him of this sudden turn of events. He was bewildered to say the least and probably a little hesitant to believe. It truly was a miracle. I'm sure you know that people don't just get sick like that and magically heal up the next morning.

My doctor postponed the emergency ER "reservation" he made for me. The plan was to see how the next few days went. One week later my lab report showed better health than I had ever had since my initial diagnosis. I never went to the ER after all.

All was well and I was in remission for a year and a half. This is where the cycle comes in. I lost self-control, and certain choices I made caused a relapse. After being in remission for so long, I figured I could be less strict with my diet. I started sneaking sugar on a regular basis. Then I attended a birthday party after moving to Hawaii. I was the new younger girl and I wanted to fit in. That night I ate enough sugar to make any human being sick.

That did me in. My labs were already showing that my health was declining and I went downhill really fast. I regretted the choices I made for nearly the next two years. Never again will I make bad decisions like I did that night.

This cycle is one that all Crohn's patients have to struggle with. When you start getting better, you want to eat more foods that aren't good for you and you push your body. I find that I start to become less concerned about my well-being. Eating delicious food becomes more of a priority than eating healthy food. Staying up late with friends seems like an okay idea more and more often. Exercise is no longer a consistent part of my daily schedule.

This is a pattern of destruction. I seem to "forget" to take all my supplements. The next thing I know the cycle begins again. I start to have occasional pain. Then finally I realize I am slipping back towards a relapse. I abandon all unhealthy eating and return to my strict diet. Oftentimes it's too late, and the Crohn's is already fully active again.

A great aspect about the SCD diet is you are in control of the cycle. As long as you follow the diet, you can stay well. It's up to you to be healthy. If you start making poor choices and eating illegal foods, you'll have to deal with the costs.

Since I started the diet I haven't slipped up. For four years I've had health. Being in remission has made me wonder a few things. Questions have been running through my mind. *Is this remission going to last forever? Will the Crohn's come back as soon as I stop the diet?*

Then there is a huge question that I have not dared to let cross my mind in years.

Is there a cure?

CHAPTER 12

A FLICKER OF HOPE

Until now, I had scarcely allowed myself to believe that there is hope for a cure. But nothing is impossible. In the history of humankind, there have been many illnesses and diseases that were thought to be incurable. Time and technology, however, proved that to be untrue. A cure for Crohn's may be much closer than we think.

Recently, I discovered an intriguing article. I asked a doctor about it to see if it was legitimate. The doctor told me it was really something the medical community was looking into. Naturally I was excited and read it right away.

The article has to do with the link between paratuberculosis and Crohn's. The more I read, the more I was convinced that a cure is not far off. More and more pieces of the puzzle are starting to fall into place.

If you're interested, do a quick Google search of Crohn's and paratuberculosis. The idea is that a bacterium called *Mycobacterium avium subspecies paratuberculosis* (MAP) causes a disease called Johne's in cows. This disease, which occurs in cattle, is very similar to Crohn's. It's possible that the bacteria are passed on to humans from milk. The article I read is called "Paratuberculosis and Crohn's Disease: Got Milk?" It discusses all the pros and cons of this theory pretty well.

It definitely makes sense to me that Crohn's is bacteria related. By going to Mexico I disturbed the internal balance of bacteria in my gut. That explains why the SCD diet has worked for me. If Crohn's is caused by bacteria, it could be cured by killing the bacteria.

I now see light at the end of the tunnel and have begun accepting that this may no longer be a lifelong disease. Paratuberculosis may not hold the answers to a cure for Crohn's, but I do believe there is one. Slowly more people are discovering relief in various diets. There have also been advances in different types of medication and treatment. It is only a matter of time until everything comes together. I moved from Maui to go to school in Minnesota for an education in bioscience. I am currently in college pursuing a career in medicine. I am joining the medical community to help discover a way to cure this disease.

Even if the cure does not come in our generation, hope is certain. You can always have hope for the future. For now the SCD diet has completely changed me and given me a new life. When Crohn's hit everything changed, now I have regained what I lost and more. One of the reasons I chose to put my wave picture on the cover of this book is because it is symbolic to me.

For years I was really sick. I sat on the shore and watched my friends and family play in the water.

~~~

"Krystal, come in the water!" My friends called out excitedly to me.

Sitting in the hot sand, I glanced at my dad. "Can I please go in?"

"You shouldn't go in. There are bad bacteria in the ocean and if you accidentally swallow the water it will make you even sicker."

"I won't swallow any, I promise!" My protests were to no avail.

My dad shook his head no. I watched the ocean with longing as the hot sun beat down.

~~~

Now that I've been on the SCD diet for four years, let me give you an idea of how my trips to the beach go.

~~~

The roar of the waves reaches my ears. Wildly I run down to the sand to see what the conditions are like.

"Yewwww!" I let out a scream of excitement.

One of my guy friends whistles. "Wow! Look at those ten footers!" Glassy waves are breaking on the shore. Grabbing my camera I run and dive into the water as a large wave roars above my head.

"Outside!" One of my friends yells, warning me of another wave approaching.

With my camera on, I swim towards the wall of water getting sucked up into it. As the water crashes over my head, I quickly take the shot looking through the barrel of the wave.

Three hours later my best friend yells from the shore, "Krystal, are you coming out yet?"

I look at her. "Are you kidding me?"

I break out into happy laughter just before the next wave crashes on me, sending me tumbling. *I love being in the waves. Never again will I sit on the shore.*

~~~

As a result of overcoming sickness, I've become bolder. If I hadn't been sick I might have just been another girl who sits on the shore. But since I missed out on so much, now that I'm well I try to live to the fullest. The meaning of the saying "carpe diem" is to urge someone to make the most of the present time. Maybe Crohn's will come back and maybe it won't; either way I'm going to live.

The second way Crohn's has changed me is through my eating habits. My diet is so much healthier. Although I'm not allowed to eat junk food, there are some foods that I can eat now that I couldn't when I was sick. For example, now I can eat salads, nuts, and berries without a problem. These are foods I used to miss and they're all healthy!

~~~

My dad was cutting strawberries up by the sink. They were so big and red and perfect looking. I wished I could have one.

"Could I just have one please?" I begged.

"It's still pretty early in the diet," he cautioned.

"I don't care; I haven't tasted a berry in so long," I insisted.

"Alright, Krystal."

The delicious taste filled my mouth and my twelve-year-old self was overjoyed. I ran around the house hollering, "I ate a strawberry! The most amazing strawberry in the world!"

~~~

That was probably a few months into the diet. Now I eat strawberries almost every morning for breakfast. Even though I have to give up sugar and bread, I can eat healthy food and be symptom free! Having the self-control to eat right has been one of the best things that has ever happened to me. Crohn's has benefited me in other ways as well.

My perspective towards students who have a hard time with school has also changed. I have always been a strong student and have helped my fellow classmates. After struggling with reading from prednisone, I finally understood what it was like to be the one who needs help. This has motivated me to continue to assist any students who need it.

~~~

My cell phone rang for the umpteenth time that night and I knew why. Finals were coming up.

Picking it up, I said hello.

"Hey, have you done the history study guide yet?" a student asked on the other line.

"No, but I'll start tonight after I study for the chemistry test," I replied.

"Thank you so much," she replied gratefully. "Oh, and do you think we could Skype later in the week and go over some of the information?"

"Yes, of course!" I answered and then hung up.

The clock read 12:30 AM. Yawning, I struggled to stay awake. "Wake up, Krystal!" I yelled at myself out loud. It was no use. My eyes drooped closed. Giving up, I set my alarm for 5:30 AM and fell asleep with all my books still open in my bed.

~~~

Lastly the disease has changed me by making me stronger. I no longer worry about problems average teenagers worry about. I'm not concerned as much with what others think or say about me.

~~~

My friends whispered to each other after a girl walked by us in the hallway.

I rolled my eyes. I wasn't really listening to the gossip.

"Can you believe that?" they asked me after they were done talking.

"What?" I asked.

"Krystal, were you even listening?" they asked annoyed.

"Not really," I replied and then walked away. I wondered about the girl who had a bad reputation. I wondered what kind of difficulties she has been through to make her act that way. And I wished I could help her.

~~~

Crohn's has made me mature as a person. I try not to hurt anyone or leave anyone out. And even if people insult me, I try my best to not let it get me down, and instead show them kindness. After all, you never know what someone's life is really like. I'm sure that, if some of the students I went to school with read this book, they'd be quite surprised.

Trying to treat people with as much respect as I can has been a goal. That doesn't mean I am always super nice; several times I have had to confront people for their behavior. That is part of life.

I'm not saying Crohn's is a blessing, and I'm not saying it's a curse. It's simply a part of each of our lives as patients. Crohn's will change you, so embrace it and try to use it to become a better person. No matter how sick you may be at times, don't be discouraged. Hang on to that flicker of hope that things will get better. Crohn's isn't your whole life, even though at times it may seem like it. Whatever damage the Crohn's has done in your life, go back and rebuild. Strive for physical and emotional healing.

And never give up, because hope is certain.

Posters of my wave photography are available for purchase through my Krystal Hawaii Photography Facebook page. I am donating 50% of the profits to the Crohn's & Colitis Foundation of America in order to fund more research. (Please mention *Hope Is Certain* at the time of purchase.)

It is my desire that this poster will inspire you to remember that hope is certain and you *can* have the life you dreamed of.

Printed in Poland
by Amazon Fulfillment
Poland Sp. z o.o., Wrocław

52436617R00075